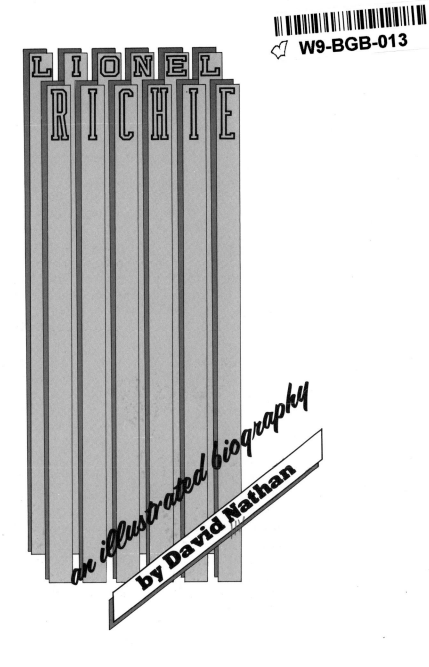

LIONEL RICHIE

an illustrated biography

by David Nathan

McGRAW-HILL BOOK COMPANY

New York · St Louis · San Francisco · Bogotá · Guatemala · Hamburg · Lisbon
Madrid · Mexico · Montreal · Panama · Paris · San Juan
São Paolo · Tokyo · Toronto

Copyright © 1985 by David Nathan

All rights reserved. Printed in England. Except as
permitted under the Copyright Act of 1976, no
part of this publication may be reproduced or
distributed in any form or by any means, or stored
in a data base or retrieval system, without the
prior written permission of the publisher.
First American edition 1985.

1 2 3 4 5 6 7 8 9 D O C D O C 8 7 6 5 4

ISBN 0-07-046030-2

Library of Congress Catalog Card Number 84-29686

Library of Congress Cataloging in Publication Data

Nathan, David.
    Lionel Richie: an illustrated biography.

    1. Richie, Lionel. 2. Singers – United States –
Biography. I. Title.

ML420.R524N4   1985   784.5'5'00924 **[B]**   84-29686
ISBN 0-07-046030-2

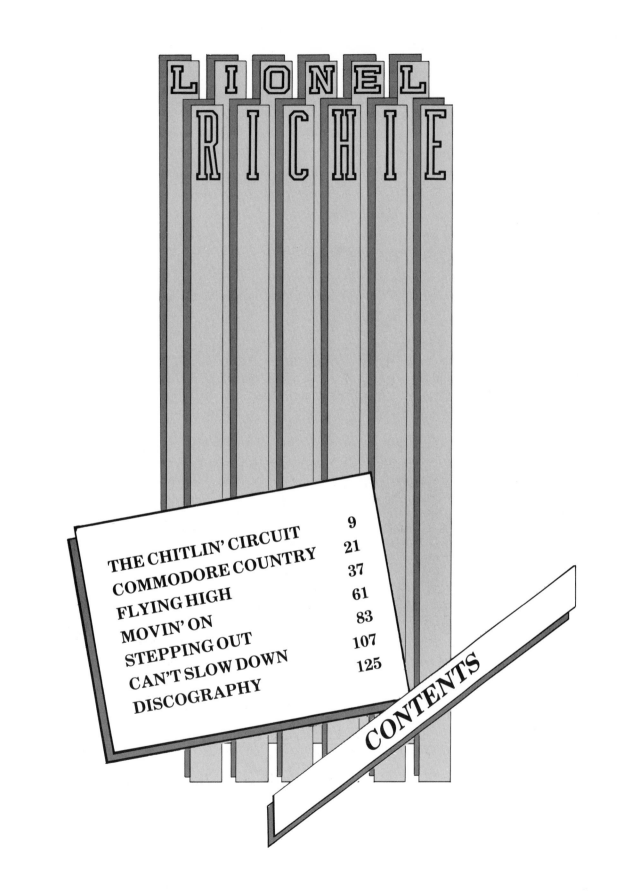

LIONEL RICHIE

CONTENTS

THE CHITLIN' CIRCUIT   9

COMMODORE COUNTRY   21

FLYING HIGH   37

MOVIN' ON   61

STEPPING OUT   83

CAN'T SLOW DOWN   107

DISCOGRAPHY   125

David Nathan has been a contributor to the British music magazine, *Blues & Soul,* since 1970. From 1975-81, he was their New York editor and interviewed almost every major black entertainer including Earth, Wind and Fire, Roberta Flack, Quincy Jones, Dionne Warwick, Aretha Franklin, Diana Ross and The Commodores.

He has written biographies for record companies on such artists as Luther Vandross, and The Staple Singers and continues to contribute feature stories to *Blues and Soul.* David is currently working on projects with Maurice White, Dionne Warwick and Impact Studios. David lives both in London and in Los Angeles.

ABOUT THE AUTHOR

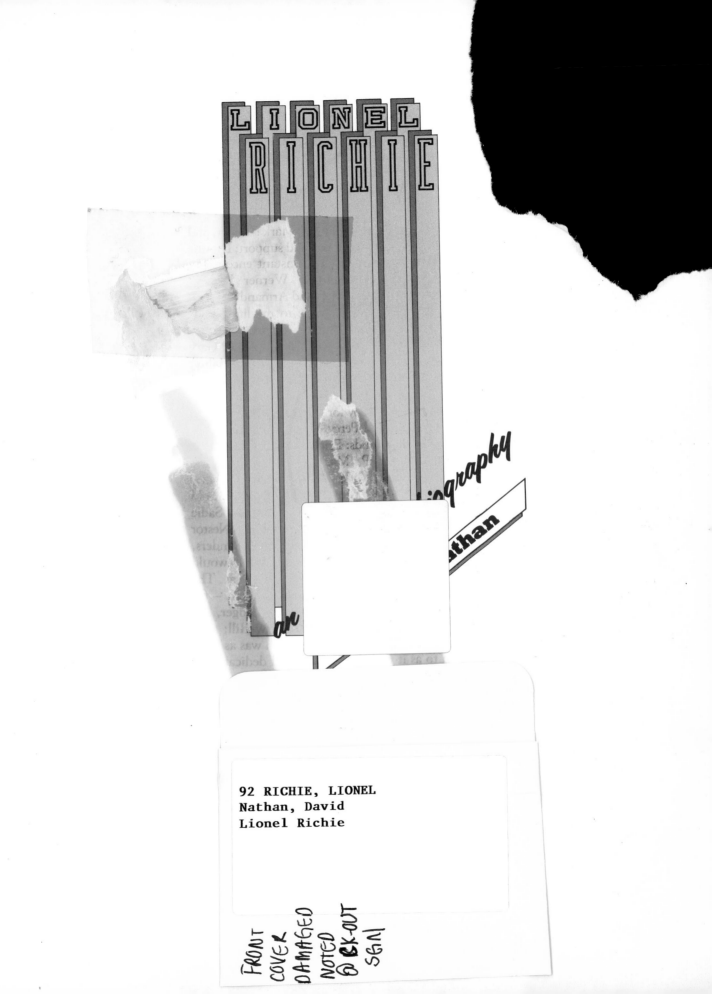

LIONEL
RICHIE

...iography
...athan

an

FRONT
COVER DAMAGED
NOTED
@ CK-OUT
SGN

I should like to thank my father, Mark Nathan, and my sister, Sylvia, for their love and support; Dionne Warwick for her inspiration, constant encouragement, friendship and music; Werner Erhard, Laurel Scheaf, Tirzah Cohen and Armand di Carlo for the difference they've made to my life; Tracy Goss and all at Impact Studios for providing the space of love in which to get this completed; Gary and Shatema Byrd for their love and hospitality; Maurice White for his inspiration and guidance; Roberta Flack for her words of wisdom; Doris ("Just One Look") Troy for the years of friendship; Arthur Freeman and Percy Bryant for their spiritual strength; my friends: Eric B, Chuck S, Alan W, Tommie G, Pam P, Mas K, Seth W, in Los Angeles and New York; Paul, Critch, Patricia, Glen, Ray, Aly, Jeff, Tony, Ray Shell, P P Arnold and the gang at *Blues & Soul* in London; and Sadie and Mrs Morgan for their great cooking; Nestor Figueroa – so much for Pharaohs!; David Sanders, without whose word processor this book would never have been started; all the folks at The Garage, The Catch, The Rage and The Lift – for exercise; John Brown at Virgin; Cat Ledger, my ruthless editor; Tom Miller at McGraw-Hill; and, of course, Lionel Richie's music which was as great to listen to as it was to write about. I dedicate this book to the memory of my mother, Frances – with much love.

David Nathan
London
December 1984

ACKNOWLEDGEMENTS

It is a privilege to have been asked to write the introduction to this book. Lionel "B", as he is affectionately known to his friends, is one of the finest singer/songwriters of the decade, and in my opinion will be known as such for many years to come.

Lionel's songs, be it the beauty and poignancy of 'Hello', the celebration of 'All Night Long', or the tenderness of 'Truly', have touched people everywhere. I have had great pleasure singing some of these songs; and you too will have found enormous pleasure listening to Lionel's music. Now you can get to know more about Lionel "B", the person, in the pages of this book.

Enjoy! I did.

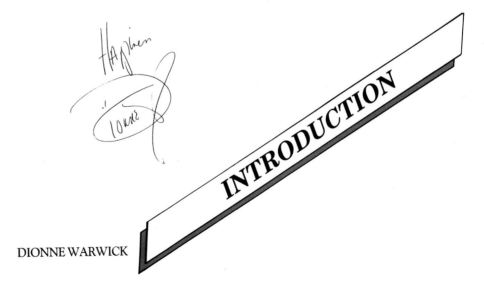

DIONNE WARWICK

CHAPTER

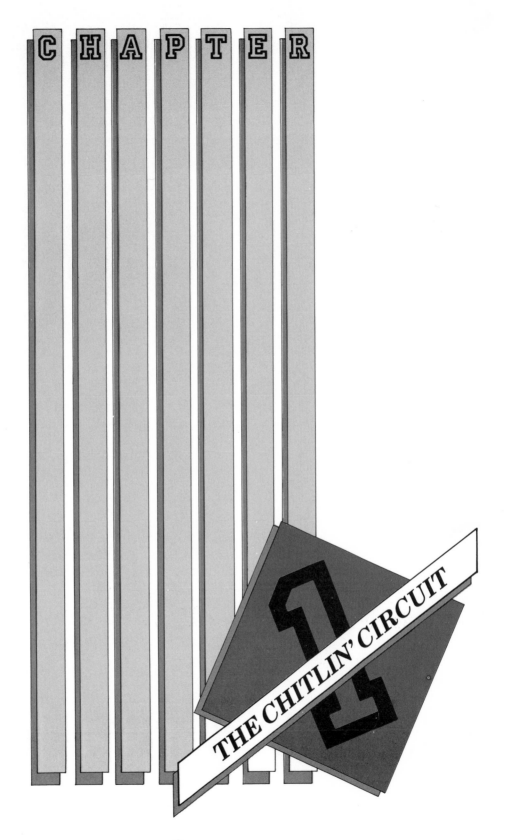

1

THE CHITLIN' CIRCUIT

Lionel Brockman Richie Jr. was born in Tuskegee, Alabama, in June 1949, right on the campus of the Tuskegee Institute – the most prestigious black university in the South – where his grandmother was the choir director. The son of a retired army captain, Lyonel, and an elementary school-teacher, Alberta, Lionel was, by all accounts, a good student during his high school years. His original career plans were certain: he wanted to go into the ministry and become a priest. "I had a strict, middle-class family upbringing, especially since my father was a military man. So it was always about a respectable career – the notion of being an entertainer would not have gone down well with my family."

Music, however, was never too far away. His uncle Bertram, a big-band player from New York who had been an arranger for Duke Ellington, gave Lionel his first saxophone; and his grandmother made sure he practised the keyboard rigorously. Lionel had to attend all the school's musical activities – "all the ballets and symphonies too."

After high school, Lionel moved on to the Tuskegee Institute. Although he had never been an athletic champion at school, he got to the Institute on a tennis scholarship. (Lionel later participated in various celebrity tennis tournaments with other members of The Commodores; he also befriended tennis star Jimmy Connors – who made a musical appearance on his first solo album in 1982.)

Lionel recollects his college years during the mid-Sixties: "The funny thing about me was that I was never a part of the in-crowd at college. And I was hopeless when it came to dating girls. The first time I saw the lady who was to become my wife, Brenda Harvey, she was marching as a majorette at a football game and I didn't even know how to go about asking her out!"

Although he may have been shy with girls, Lionel was no slouch with his studies and his original plans to become an Episcopal minister were well in progress by 1967 – "I was going to study for two years at Tuskegee before going on to Wyoming Seminary" – when he met fellow students Thomas McClary, newly arrived from Florida, and William King.

McClary also came from a musical family – his brother was a college band leader, his four sisters sang together as The McClarys. Originally a ukelele player, he had switched to the guitar just before meeting Lionel. King had been a member of his local Baptist choir, and originally attended Hampton Institute on a music scholarship (playing classical trumpet in the college band) before coming to Tuskegee Institute.

Pursuing an obvious interest in music with his sax playing, Lionel teamed up with King and McClary in a campus group McClary had formed – "as a way to meet the ladies!" Known as The Mystics, the trio could frequently be found rehearsing in Lionel's grandmother's basement. Lionel's musical influences at that time were diverse: he listened to jazz musicians, like Miles Davis, Stanley Turrentine and Herbie Hancock, as well as to The Beatles, James Taylor, and Crosby, Stills and Nash. He also tuned in to the local Tuskegee country station, but the rhythmic sound of funk and r&b was ever-present. "Thomas and William first heard me playing some riffs from a James Brown song, 'Cold Sweat', and that's how I became part of the group," Lionel recalls.

One of the group's first public performances was in a talent show at college. The line-up was Richie, King and McClary, drummer Andre Callaghan and a bass player known as "Railroad" (who was also lead singer for the group). Trumpet-player King remembers: "It was one of those shows where, no matter how good or how bad you were, the audience threw things at you. We decided it would be a little different for us: we'd get a standing ovation so that no one would even think about throwing anything at all. We had two songs ready – both uptempo James Brown numbers, hits of the day. Well, even before the curtain went up, Richie and Railroad had split, leaving the three of us behind. It truly wasn't one of our better performances but I left to find Richie before the pelting began!"

The Mystics went on to do some local high school proms and more college dates before joining forces in February 1968 with The Jays, another local group who were considered hot stuff in Tuskegee at the time. The Jays were led by keyboardist Milan Williams, a native of Okolona, Mississippi, who had come to the Tuskegee Institute to study industrial engineering, and the line-up had included Michael Gilbert on bass and Jimmy Johnson on saxophone. When the groups merged, a change of name seemed in order. Lionel remembers: "We had all kinds of wonderful ideas – 'The Fantastic Soulful Six', 'The Mighty Wonders'. In fact, we almost broke up just trying to come up with a new name. We finally turned to the dictionary and William King stuck his finger on a page and we came up with 'commodore', an old naval term describing someone who ranks between captain and admiral. We were lucky because that word was real close to the word 'commode' and we might have ended up as 'The Commodes', performing in suits made out of toilet paper!"

Still in college, the group started doing shows in neighbouring states (Mississippi and Louisiana), as well as in nearby towns like Montgomery, gaining a good reputation for their stage show in the process. According to King, they played for between $15 and $20 dollars a night "and as many fish sandwiches as we could eat!" During this period Lionel decided that becoming a priest was not for him. "When I first joined the group, little did I know that rock and roll was going to get a hold on me the way it did. By the end of my freshman year, I knew music was going to be my life. So I went to the bishop and just told him that I was more interested in making music my ministry. When I let my family know the same thing, my father just refused to talk to me. He figured I'd become a hooligan and that being in showbusiness was about as far from being respectable as I could get."

Undeterred, Lionel spent weekends and college holidays performing with The Commodores. He continued his studies in economics (although he didn't actually graduate until May 1974). The other members of the group were also completing their education: Williams and King were studying electronics, McClary business administration.

Just as The Commodores were beginning to

Religion has always been a major influence in Lionel's life; he is seen here at a service in his home town of Tuskegee. From left: Ronald LaPread, Thomas McClary, Shirley and William King, Brenda and Lionel Richie, Gwen and Milan Williams, Walter "Clyde" Orange and Benny Ashburn.

make a little headway, Lionel met Brenda Harvey, still in her first year at college. It may have been love at first sight for Lionel but, as he remembers, she wasn't exactly bowled over by him: "I was very nervous about asking her out, so much so that I ended up asking a friend of mine to introduce us. If I remember correctly, she was with one of her girlfriends at the time and I bought her a soda – but I was tongue-tied and I just didn't know what to say to her! Thankfully, I finally got up the nerve to ask her out. I'd had three girlfriends before I met Brenda but I knew she was my real college sweetheart right from the start. To be honest, though, it took about three years for us to really get to know and appreciate each other fully and,

during that time, I played it straight – no funny business. Brenda fell in love with this shy guy, the guy who didn't know how to say 'I love you', who ended up sending her notes with those three little words written a hundred times over. We fell in love before the hits, before the fame, before the fortune. She was there before The Commodores were known around the world, before anyone knew who I was."

However, Lionel and the other Commodores were determined the world would get to hear about them; they were filled with ambition. Popular music in the US during the Sixties had gone through several phases. Black girl groups – The Shirelles, The Chiffons, The Ronettes, The Cookies and so on – had dominated the music scene from 1961 to 1963. The British "invasion", spearheaded by The Beatles and The Rolling Stones, had hit the country in 1964 and their songs were still topping the charts in 1968. Motown, from its early beginnings in Detroit with hits by The Miracles, Barrett Strong and, later on, Mary Wells, Marvin Gaye and "Little" Stevie Wonder, had arrived in full force. Acts such as The Supremes, The Four Tops, The Temptations and Martha & The Vandellas provided the excitement and finger-snappin' music that became known throughout the world as "The Motown Sound" or "The Sound Of Young America".

At the other end of the spectrum, Stax Records in Memphis was producing a funkier, more "down-home" sound – the real base for what became known as soul music – with artists like Otis Redding and Sam & Dave. Meanwhile, Aretha Franklin, a young woman from Detroit with a strong background in gospel music, had exploded on to charts across the world with what was to become a soul classic, 'Respect'. James Brown, the "Godfather Of Soul", continued to provide consistency with his distinctive sound and Sly Stone, a former DJ from San Francisco, was fusing rhythm and blues and rock to create a sound that would influence the shape of popular music for at least a decade. However, by 1968, sophisticated black acts such as Dionne Warwick and The Fifth Dimension, were making regular appearances on the pop charts. For the first time, Las Vegas seemed within reach of contemporary black entertainers. Motown, in particular, was grooming stars such as Diana Ross and The Supremes to appear at classy nightclubs like the famed Copacabana in New York.

Nevertheless, the options open to any black group just starting out in 1968 were limited. The famous "chitlin'" circuit (named after a soul food delicacy served in neighbourhood clubs and bars) was still the entry to stardom, and that meant two or three shows a night in less than the best possible conditions. Clubs were frequently cramped, with tiny dressing-rooms and little room to move on stage. Road tours were gruelling; transportation was often no more than a broken-down bus or van – "not exactly your scenic route model!" as one veteran performer commented.

The Commodores, however, were not interested in becoming just another black group caught in the same old syndrome. "We wanted to know why a group like The Temptations with all their hit records couldn't sell out a 25,000-seat stadium and yet Led Zeppelin could show up and within twenty-four hours there'd be no tickets left," William King recalls. "We wanted to know how come no black act had achieved that in 1968, so we went to see every concert that hit the area."

They studied the music of the day with great diligence: "I even did a 200-page essay on The Beatles!" remembers King. "I discovered that there were several factors involved in making it to the kind of level that The Beatles had. It took good management, good music and, above all, teamwork; plus that extra special ingredient, charisma. You saw that every time The Beatles were on stage: they clicked together. So we figured that, for The Commodores to make it that big, we needed to have the same kind of close-knit relationship with each other. It took quite a few lengthy talking sessions to get to that. We each had to know what the other was up to, what each one of us wanted out of being in the group and, frankly, whether we loved or hated each other!" King says that the group developed such a tight interaction that "a nod of the head on stage, a certain look and you'd know what to do, you knew what was going on over there with the other guys."

The group made their first venture into the recording studios in New York at Grove Sound Studios with r&b producer Jerry Williams (also known as "Swampp Dogg") in February 1969 after Williams had visited Tuskegee and seen the group perform there. William King remembers the first time they met the eccentric producer: "He was wearing a bright green shirt! Shoes, socks, pants and shirt and jacket – all lime green! And that shocked me! I know I'm from Alabama, but this was a bit far out by anybody's standards." The group recorded a total of nine songs for Cotillion Records, a subsidiary of Atlantic Records, but the results were disappointing. Most of the material was unoriginal

From left: Walter "Clyde" Orange, William King, Ronald LaPread, Lionel Richie, Milan Williams and Thomas McClary.

and only one song, 'Keep On Dancin' ', was released as a single. Lionel reflects: "It was almost like an audition in recording for us. We recorded everything at the same time, there was no overdubbing and we did songs like Johnnie Taylor's 'Who's Making Love' and The Intruders' 'Cowboys To Girls'. We were happy enough considering this was our first shot in the studios, but we knew somehow that something better was possible."

Spurred on by their goal to become "the world's No.1 group, the 'black Beatles' ", The Commodores headed for "the Big Apple" once again, this time not to record but to perform. It was the summer of 1969. Jimmy Johnson had been asked to

leave the group, and they were now a sextet. "We were six young kids," remembers King, "cocky and headstrong, ready to take the world and New York in particular by storm." On arrival, the group directed their steps to Harlem, the centre of the city's black community, to the YMCA on 135th Street and 7th Avenue.

"We ended up sharing one room by turning the bed lengthwise, all six of us sleeping across it!" recalls King. Around the corner from the "Y" was Small's Paradise, a legendary rhythm and blues club of the day, where The Commodores decided to try their luck. "Here we were, six country boys, and we marched right in to see Pete Smalls, the owner. We told him we wanted to work in his club and he just stood back and stared at us! We told him: 'Whatever you need, we've got it.' He pointed to the door and told us in no uncertain terms: 'There you go, use it!' End of our first opportunity to make it in the big time in New York."

But The Commodores' troubles were far from over. While the group had been talking to Pete Smalls, an intruder had visited their van and stolen their uniforms and equipment. The thief then showed up to resell them their property and, a few days later, another "visitor" broke in to The Commodores' "luxury suite" at the "Y" and stole everything that was left. By this time, The Commodores were discouraged and disheartened, wondering if they were really going to take New York by storm after all. "It was rough," William King recalls. "We had no work and our money was fast running out. On top of that, we had next to no equipment or clothes left."

Things began to look up, however, when Milan Williams remembered a man he'd met during an earlier visit to New York when the group had performed at a benefit show held at New York's Town Hall. (It had been arranged by the Tuskegee Institute as part of a musical exchange programme with other black colleges.) The man in question was Benny Ashburn, a marketing executive with Dewars, a whisky manufacturing company, who had done publicity work for the benefit. Benny had been impressed with The Commodores' performance and had told them that if they were ever back in New

York, they should look him up. He responded to Milan's call by showing up at the YMCA; and when he saw how committed the group were to making their debut in New York, he moved them out of the YMCA and into his uptown apartment on 135th Street and Lenox Terrace, just around the corner from the "Y". "We knew the guy had to be all right. He didn't know us from Adam and yet he was willing to take us in."

Ashburn immediately set about arranging a performance for The Commodores; he contacted Pete Smalls who agreed to give them a slot on a Monday night – traditionally audition night at his club. The Commodores, elated at the opportunity to perform at the venue, called all the Tuskegee students they knew in New York, asking them to bring their families and friends to the show. Monday nights weren't usually busy at Small's Paradise, so when the club filled out to hear The Commodores, Pete Smalls decided to book the group for a three-week stay. This led to a further two-month booking at the club, giving The Commodores their first big break and Lionel his nickname. "I kept some of the money from that very first show," remembers Lionel, "and that's how I got the nickname 'Jack Benny', the comedian who was always known for his miserly ways!"

Just before they began the two-month gig, drummer Michael Gilbert was drafted into the military service. The obvious replacement was Walter "Clyde" Orange, a native of Jacksonville, Florida, who had studied at Alabama State University. When Orange returned home to Jacksonville after graduating from college, Gilbert had approached him about joining the group. At the time, Orange had declined the offer but he remembers that "when the phone rang three days later, I knew who was on the other end." In September 1969, towards the end of their trip up North while performing in Atlantic City, bass player Andre Callaghan decided to join the Navy. Ronald LaPread, who had studied at Jackson State University in Mississippi and knew several members of the group, replaced him. This was now the final line-up of The Commodores – until Lionel left the group in 1982 – with Lionel on sax and vocals, Milan Williams on keyboards,

William King on Trumpet, Thomas McClary on guitar, Walter "Clyde" Orange on drums and Ronald LaPread on bass.

The group now had Benny Ashburn working with them as their manager. When they formalized their business association in 1969, The Commodores and Ashburn formed The Commodores Entertainment Corporation; the seven were equal partners, democratically voting on all major decisions affecting the group's career. Ashburn had a master's degree in marketing from New York University, and a successful career with Schenley Industries, Pepsi-Cola, and then Dewar's behind him; he used this background in business to create a seven-year plan for The Commodores. It was Benny Ashburn, more than anyone else, who was responsible for the emergence of The Commodores, and his career guidance was to prove invaluable.

Just before they returned to Tuskegee in the autumn of 1969, Benny booked the group into a showcase at entertainer Lloyd Price's Turntable Club on 50th Street and Broadway in the heart of New York's Tin Pan Alley. There, says Milan Williams, "we got to show off our new line-up and the new sound we had created." That year, The Commodores spent almost every weekend travelling to gigs in places like Boston and New York (they appeared at the famed Cheetah Club on 52nd Street), Virginia and The Carolinas, frequently playing at local colleges.

In the summer vacation of 1970, the group made their first trip overseas. Playing on the liner S.S.France en route to the French Riviera, the group met famed television host Ed Sullivan. Ed was so impressed with the group's performance that he actually booked them to appear on his show, although his unexpected death later that year meant that the group never appeared on the show. When they arrived in the South of France, the group played at several different venues, quickly becoming popular with local audiences. William King recalls: "We performed at one club called the Acu-Acu in a place near Cannes and then in a resort club in St Tropez. This was a very, very rich place. But it did a lot for us because it let us know we could bridge the gap between different cultures as well as different

The Commodores became known as one of the hardest-working bands in pop music during the Seventies, as a result of their hectic touring schedule. They performed with numerous other popular black acts, and are pictured here with The Emotions.

age groups since most of the people in the audience in France were significantly older than those we were playing to back home in the States." This exposure helped The Commodores to entertain a very cosmopolitan audience, a factor which was to be important in the acceptance of the group's music a few years later.

In November 1970, Benny Ashburn secured another booking for the group at a black lawyers' convention at Small's Paradise; this was to become a major turning-point in The Commodores' career. The group, however, nearly missed the show altogether, as William King remembers: "We had planned to drive up from Tuskegee the previous night as usual but this particular journey was

fraught with incidents! When we got to Atlanta, one of the tyres blew, followed in quick succession by another two, so we had to get out and push the van to a gas station. We made it to Richmond, Virginia, when a fleet of police on motorcycles came screeching up. Apparently, there had been a local bank robbery and three of the guys fit the descriptions for the robbers! Well, we sorted that one out and we were on our way again – with three new tyres and $20 left.

"Fate was certainly being unkind to us that day because, of course, the fourth tyre blew. We made it on the three tyres to the nearest gas station when, would you believe, the gas ran out. Since we'd spent our last money on replacing the tyre, we were now really stuck. There we were in New Jersey, no gas

From left: Randy Jackson, Milan Williams, Thomas McClary, Tito Jackson, Jermaine Jackson, William King, Billy Preston and Lionel Richie.

and the show due to start just a couple of hours later. We tried to bargain with the gas attendant but all we had to trade with was our instruments and he wasn't interested in amplifiers or guitars! We finally persuaded him to speak to Benny. We still don't know what Benny said but, whatever it was, it worked because the guy gave us some money and gas and we made it to the City just thirty minutes late! We were hot, sweaty, tired and hungry but we set up our equipment and did one hell of a show."

It just so happened that they were spotted at the gig by Suzanne De Passe, from Motown Records, who had been invited to the show by her sister Jean, a friend of Benny Ashburn. Suzanne had been with the company in Detroit for a couple of years and was working at that time with The Jackson Five. Natives of Gary, Indiana, who had been brought to the company's attention by Gladys Knight and Diana Ross, The J5 had caught the public's imagination with 'I Want You Back' and 'The Love You Save'; they needed a strong opening act for their first national tour, due to begin in December. A couple of weeks after seeing The Commodores at Small's Paradise, De Passe rang Benny Ashburn offering the group an opportunity to open for The Jackson Five on their first eight dates. This, as it turned out, was to be the beginning of a long association between Motown and The Commodores (an association which has lasted to the present day both for the group and for Lionel as a solo artist). More importantly, the tour provided The Commodores with their first real exposure to large audiences.

20

CHAPTER

21

COMMODORE COUNTRY

Playing on those first dates with The Jackson Five in December 1970, The Commodores had the opportunity to glimpse life in the big league. That first show provided them with a lesson in professionalism.

"One of the first things I found out," says Lionel, "was the importance of being on time for everything. Motown trained their acts in that kind of discipline and it paid off – you'd never hear anyone say anything about their acts not showing up or being late. I also discovered the importance of having the right people around – people you could trust, people you could count on. The whole experience of being around The Jacksons and Motown affected me a great deal in the way I related to myself as a professional entertainer."

"Before the show," remembers Lionel, "we had a group meeting and we decided that we were going to do a 'light' show. We didn't want to embarrass this group of kids – you've got to remember that The Jackson Five were hardly into their teens at the time. So we said we wouldn't play full out, we wouldn't do a 'hard' show. We did a couple of nice warm-up numbers and a few good tunes but nothing spectacular. We came off stage satisfied that we'd put in a good performance, and there was little Michael – he must have been about ten or eleven – running around playing 'pat-a-cake' and pinching people. Then the stage darkened and when the lights went up this same little kid was singing his behind off! The audience went wild – The J5 were tearing up the place with their energy and dynamism. So we had another Commodores' meeting that night and realized that the kids, as we called them, had killed us and we'd better pull out all the stops for the rest of the tour!"

The Commodores, however, didn't have the wealth of original material The J5 had. Their repertoire consisted of a mixture of Top 10 pop and r&b songs of the day, such as Glen Campbell's 'Wichita Lineman', Seals & Crofts' 'Summer Breeze' and The Temptations' 'Cloud Nine'. Nevertheless, the group's show elicited a warm response from audiences and Lionel and The Commodores began to see the possibility of a long-term career in music.

They were booked to appear on the second Jackson Five tour in the spring and summer of 1971 playing stadiums across the US, from Hawaii to New York, for a total of 42 days. They discovered on that tour that it was going to take determination, commitment and, above all, hard work. Lionel's attitude to making money out of music changed. He was on hand on one occasion when The Jacksons picked up a check for $180,000 for a night's work. "I saw a lot of money being made and poured back into building an empire. In fact, I saw an empire being built out of an empire."

The J5's performance at Madison Square Garden in New York, during their second tour, on 31 July, was a major turning-point for Lionel. "There I was backstage at this world-famous stadium and Michael turns to me and says, 'Look, we've sold out Madison Square Garden, just the two of us, The Jacksons and The Commodores!' Now, I knew really The Jacksons were the ones who'd done it but it gave me a vision for what I wanted to achieve with The Commodores, for what I could see for the first time might be possible for us." It was going to take a few more years before The Commodores were headlining their own show at The Garden, but their first major national review, which appeared in *Variety,* was encouraging: "What you see and hear is what you want more of, as indicated by the tremendous response from the capacity crowd to The Commodores, a dynamic group from Alabama."

On stage, The Commodores provided a special brand of excitement and energy that made them one of the hottest bands of the Seventies.

24

recording attempts before this goal was realized. Funk – with its heavy bass lines, simple lyrics, wah-wah guitars, dominant horn parts and vast appeal to black record-buyers throughout the United States – had emerged in the Seventies in the music of black groups like The Ohio Players and War. It was decidedly not a part of the tried-and-tested Motown formula, but Motown prided itself on being ahead of the game in the music business (continuing its tradition not simply as a record company but as an institution in popular music). The Jackson Five, after all, had combined the best of r&b with pop to create the latest in a line of million-sellers for the organization.

After signing The Commodores in the spring of 1971 to the MoWest label, a newly-formed subsidiary of Motown, Suzanne De Passe matched them with a series of producers. The group did sessions with Hal Davis (who produced all of The J5 hits), Greg and Anita Poree (who worked with Eddie Kendricks after he left The Temptations), and Jeffrey Bowen (who produced The Temps in the mid-Seventies and Bonnie Pointer in the mid-Eighties for Motown). Most of the sessions proved disastrous, however, since the music The Commodores wanted to make bore little resemblance to the work that Motown's staff producers had been so successful with.

In March 1972, with the group playing 63 one-nighters on its third and final national tour with The Jackson Five, Motown finally released two sides produced by the team of Gloria Jones and Pam Sawyer. Gloria Jones was a black American soul singer who had had her own run of hits in the mid-Sixties, including the r&b classic 'Heartbeat'; she worked in the UK in the mid-Seventies where she met and later married rock star Marc Bolan. Her partner Pam Sawyer, an English housewife-turned-songwriter, had written a significant amount of material for groups like The Supremes and Gladys Knight & The Pips. ('If I Were Your Woman' was one of the latter's biggest Motown hits.)

The A-side of The Commodores' first single, a ditty entitled 'The Zoo (The Human Zoo)', was released and was vaguely reminiscent of material by War. It failed to make any significant impression on

The tour wasn't just hard work for The Commodores: it was also an opportunity to have fun. Innocent bystanders – tour managers, publicists and Motown executives – stood backstage and watched while The J5 and The Commodores attempted to outdo each other with their backstage pranks, throwing pillows and water balloons.

Fortunately, the Motown executives weren't simply watching the pillow-fights. They were listening to The Commodores and studying the audiences' reactions wherever the group performed. What Motown saw in The Commodores was the opportunity to make inroads into the growing funk market – though there would be several abortive

the charts in the US, however, even though the record did have the distinction of making the No.1 slot on the pop charts in Brazil when it was released there; it even made the lower reaches of the British pop charts (where it got as far as the No.44 spot). It was followed by another single in January 1973, 'Don't You Be Worried' – arranged and produced by Tom Baird, a Motown staff producer – which also faded into oblivion in the US. In an interview in 1977 with *Black Music,* Lionel commented: "The sounds we were making just weren't us. The company knew that they didn't have any acts comparable to folks like Earth, Wind & Fire who were just starting out at the time and they simply didn't know what to do with us. When they found out we could write our own material, they started giving it to other people to record rather than giving us a shot with it, and that was real frustrating for us."

In 1973, Lionel's name appeared for the first time on the songwriting credits of a Commodore single: he had penned the B-side of the group's third attempt at chart success, 'Are You Happy?' The song, 'There's A Song In My Heart', came out of the group's sessions with producers Clayton Ivey and Terry Woodford but, although it was in keeping with the music of the day, it was a far cry from the kind of material that, years later, saw Lionel acclaimed as one of *the* songwriters of the decade.

In the same year, what looked like another disastrous musical match turned into a hit-producing team and the start of an important relationship for Lionel. Suzanne De Passe introduced the group to James Anthony Carmichael, also from Alabama, who had already enjoyed success as an arranger at Motown on all The Jackson material produced by Hal Davis, and as producer of Gladys Knight & The Pips' singles. At their initial meeting in Motown's studios in Los Angeles, Carmichael and the group fought. It didn't look as if this team would ever get to put anything on tape, as Lionel recalls: "Here we were with our amps turned up to twelve and the windows started to rattle. Well, those windows at Motown were definitely not supposed to rattle! James was having a fit, grabbing

Lionel in the recording studio with James Carmichael (second from right).

Away from the rigours of the music business, The Commodores maintained a close friendship with one another. Lionel and fellow Commodore Ronnie LaPread are pictured (inset) at the pool table.

his coat, ready to walk out saying 'Gentlemen, gentlemen, my career!' After he heard me singing, he completely freaked out – he was used to working with groups like Gladys Knight & The Pips and here I was sounding rough and raw – 'Gentlemen, gentlemen, we must sing!' was his comment.

"You have to picture it. James was this real conservative guy – you know, neat shirt, pressed pants and all. And we were jeans and sneakers, funky and 'down-home'. So that he'd know we hadn't just arrived from the planet Mars, we played him some records by The Ohio Players and Earth, Wind & Fire so he'd get some understanding of what we were trying to do. But after he heard them, he shook his head and told us: 'Motown will never accept this kind of music.' So we just kept working with him until he saw that it was possible to sell the company on our sound."

Carmichael persevered with the group and the result was their first big hit. 'Machine Gun' started life as an instrumental written by Milan Williams; it nearly ended up with vocals, but was finally released in April 1974 in its original funky form. Lionel remembers the session well: "We cut the song piece by piece, not all at one time. I told James that I wanted to add a lot of feedback, a lot of rasp, to make it sound real 'nasty', real funky. James called in Calvin Harris, who had worked as an engineer at Motown's studios in Detroit – and then Los Angeles when the company moved there at the start of the Seventies – to work on the project. That ended up being a long-term relationship; Cal worked with us on everything from that first session on."

The session took about three days to complete and although The Commodores were satisfied with what they'd done, they had no idea of the kind of impact the record would make. "We felt that as far as the studio was concerned, we were still like children," Lionel explains. "We knew a lot about being on the road, especially after all those tours with The Jacksons, but when it came to recording, we were still a little naive. In fact, I thought you just went into the studio, turned up the amps, played and sang and that was it. I found out that there was a lot more to it than that."

'Machine Gun' gave the group its first taste of chart success. After starting out as a hit in Atlanta, Georgia – where it was the No.1 record at a local club, The Top Of The Peachtree – the record became the group's first international smash: in Nigeria, it went gold, as it did in Japan, the Philippines and Australia. In the UK, 'Machine Gun' spent 11 weeks on the pop charts, peaking at the No.20 slot in August 1974. At home in the US, where it was the group's first gold record, it became a huge hit in the r&b charts and crossed over to the Top 40 in the pop charts, hitting the No.22 spot. Motown immediately put together a compilation album, using tracks from the many different recording sessions that The Commodores had done since joining the company. This first album was something of a hotchpotch musically, although six Carmichael-Commodores-produced songs did add some degree of consistency.

After the success of the *Machine Gun* album, Motown decided that the combination of Carmichael and the group was one that worked. Carmichael, however, was not the only influence on the band: Lionel was influenced by a number of other people he met at Motown, including Norman Whitfield. Whitfield had produced several artists at Motown – Marvin Gaye and Gladys Knight & The Pips among others (he wrote the classic 'I Heard It Thru The Grapevine') – but much of his success had come with his masterful work for The Temptations. The soulful, traditional harmonies that Whitfield had produced on tunes like 'Just My Imagination', recorded in 1970, were now gone; he took the group into a whole new area, one created by Sly and his Family Stone. Purveyors of psychedelic soul, The Temptations were singing 'Papa Was A Rollin' Stone', 'Cloud Nine' and 'Runaway Child, Running Wild'. Whitfield had become an important figure in Motown's foray into the music of the day.

"Norman frequently visited our early sessions," Lionel reported in an interview with *Black Music* in 1977. "He became known as our 'record business teacher'. When he first started visiting us in the studio, we didn't actually know who he was. He'd invite members of the group to come and listen to work he was doing at the time and he coached us all in different aspects of the music business and recording. I still regard Norman as a major influence in my development because he told me something that's stayed with me: he told me that what we needed to do as a group was to take two steps back instead of rushing to take four steps forward. And that was a very valuable piece of advice because we thought we were just going to go out there and revolutionize the whole industry. So Norman was useful for us in terms of input – he'd sit there and shake his head 'yes' or 'no' when he heard what we were doing. Although our relationship had been very casual, very downbeat, Norman made a big contribution to the success of The Commodores."

The Commodores were concerned that, although 'Machine Gun' was well known, people really didn't know who the group were. They decided the solution was not to follow this first hit with another instrumental but to release a song with a distinctive vocal sound. 'I Feel Sanctified', an uptempo, raunchy, r&b song, was released in October 1974, consolidating the success of the first hit.

That year, The Commodores made their first television appearance. After their performance on Dick Clark's renowned *American Bandstand*, Lionel got the chance to talk to the host, recognised as one of the industry's top professionals. "Dick gave me a piece of advice that's stuck with me through the years. What he said in essence was that since we were providing something for the public, we should never forget that. He told us that we shouldn't make ourselves more important than the people we were performing for. He told us always to be humble and remember that any time we stopped being interested in what our fans wanted, we'd stopped getting our job done as entertainers. I've never forgotten what Dick said and I've stayed true to it through all the success and all the popularity. I know it's the public that has made us and the public that can break us, too."

1975 was an important year for The Commodores. With the overwhelming success they'd had in the Far East, the group made its first trek to Japan and the Philippines. In Manila, over a three-day

Tuskegee has always been proud of its six famous sons and Major Ford didn't mind letting the world know! The group are seen around the city's welcoming sign, erected in tribute to The Commodores in the mid-Seventies. From left: Ronald LaPread, Walter "Clyde" Orange, William King, Lionel Richie, Milan Williams and Thomas McClary.

33

Lionel with his wife, Brenda.

period, the group played to some 400,000 people at the world's largest stadium, the Araneta, breaking all attendance records (including those set by The Beatles) and causing riots everywhere they went. At home in the United States, the group was exposed to even wider audiences; they appeared with groups like The Average White Band and Earth, Wind & Fire and they opened for The Rolling Stones and Stevie Wonder. The Commodores performed at three concerts on The Stones' 1975 tour – expressly at Mick Jagger's invitation – all at the vast Spectrum stadium in Philadelphia. Response to the group, Milan Williams remembers, was initially lukewarm: "When you appear with a group like The Stones, you learn very quickly that's who the people have come to see. When we first went out on stage, the audience started to boo us off! But after a couple of numbers, they really got into our music and from then on it was smooth sailing." Sensibly, as well as their own original material, the group performed songs from the Top 10 r&b and pop hits of the day (a successful formula they'd employed on their early tours with

The Jackson Five).

The group's second album, *Caught In The Act*, was released in February 1975, and most of the material had the uptempo, groove-oriented sound their growing number of fans had come to expect. The first single released from the album, 'Slippery When Wet', was typical of the "sound of The Commodores"; it made the No.19 spot on the American pop charts at the end of June, and turned *Caught In The Act* into The Commodores' first gold album. This was just the first of many honours and awards the group began to receive. Coretta King (widow of Martin Luther King) presented the group with the prestigious "Brotherhood Citation" award during 1975. And in the autumn the group competed at the Tokyo Music Festival where they won a Bronze Award for 'Slippery When Wet'; they also picked up the "Best Singer Award" against stiff international competition.

1975 was also an important year for Lionel. It was the year that his songwriting talents really began to come to the fore, and the year he married Brenda, his college sweetheart. It was a natural decision, given the way their relationship had been going, but not one he took lightly. Marriage, he knew, was a serious business and a close friend's comments the next day didn't sit well with Lionel. "First marriage, huh?" was the friend's question. "Of course it is," was Lionel's response. "Enjoy many, many more," the friend retorted. "It took me a while to think about what my friend had said. Then I realized that what he was talking about was the risk involved in marrying an entertainer. I knew stars who'd go out on tour for months on end and come back only to find their wife had moved in with the next-door neighbour. So I did know that such things could happen and I didn't take our marriage for granted."

Lionel admits that everything wasn't always rosy with Brenda: "In fact, I did a lot of things wrong. . .I went through a period of time not wanting to spend any money – that came later on down the line when I really didn't know how much I was making. Then there'd be times I'd come home from all the touring and I'd just want to relax and be with Brenda while she wanted to go away on vacation: she'd been home all the time."

The early days of their marriage were a time of readjustment for both of them. "We went through every kind of change together – some good, some painful. You see, I was this young kid, with stars in my eyes, ready to conquer the world. And it wasn't easy living with this guy who doesn't have time to spend with you because he might be in New York or Paris at any moment."

When the subject of fidelity was discussed, Lionel vowed that he was going to remain true to his marriage vows – no easy feat when he was constantly confronted by groupies and possible one-night stands. "If a girl came up to me – no matter how good-looking – and said 'I want you to take me to bed', I couldn't go through with it. That's just the kind of guy I am. I wasn't interested in disrespecting Brenda or the vows we'd taken together."

Lionel's songs began to reflect events in his personal life, such as his marriage. The beautiful 'This Is Your Life', the second single from the *Caught In The Act* album, was the follow-up to 'Slippery When Wet'; it displayed Lionel's song-writing talents, particularly as a balladeer in what he called "the James Taylor/Carole King vein, the kind of music I love." The record was a Top 10 r&b hit when released in August 1975 and it helped establish The Commodores as more than just another funk band. Although 'I Feel Sanctified', written jointly by Lionel and The Commodores, had been recorded by the rock group Wild Cherry, 'This Is Your Life' became the first solo Richie composition to be recorded by another artist. Popular soul singer Jerry Butler cut it for a Motown album almost a year after the group had had a hit with the original version.

The group's third album, *Movin' On,* released in October (the second Commodores' album to come out in 1975), differed little from its predecessor with a predominance of the horn-laden, rhythmic grooves that had now become The Commodores' trademark. Lionel's contribution to the album, the ballad 'Sweet Love', turned out to be not only the album's high point but also the group's biggest hit to date.

From left: Milan Williams, Walter "Clyde" Orange, William King, Lionel, Thomas McClary and Ronald LaPread.

'Sweet Love', with its simple melody and pretty lyrics, was the group's first record to bridge the gap between r&b and pop audiences. It reached the No. 1 spot on the soul charts, and it was the group's first Top 10 pop success, hitting the No.5 position on *Billboard*'s Hot Hundred on Valentine's Day. Even though Lionel was still playing saxophone and sharing lead vocal duties with Walter "Clyde" Orange, 'Sweet Love' was the first song to really emphasize Lionel's unique and highly distinctive vocals, his mannered, gospel-influenced style. With 'Sweet Love', Lionel had established a sound that would propel the group to new heights.

CHAPTER

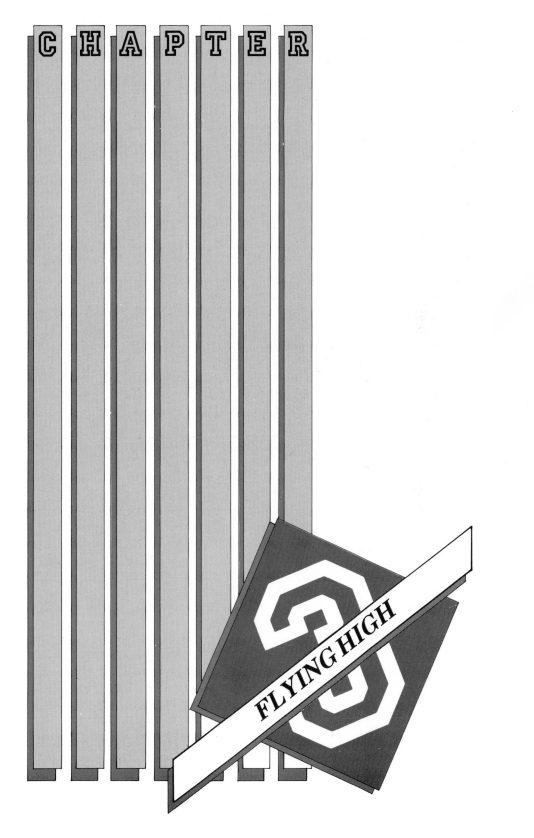

FLYING HIGH

I n 1976, with 'Sweet Love' racing up the charts, The Commodores went out on a major tour with another very popular, almost legendary, black act, The O'Jays, who had enjoyed a string of hits with songs like 'Backstabbers', 'Love Train', 'I Love Music' and 'For The Love Of Money'.

The tour began in February and ended in April. Appearing in major cities like New York, Chicago, Washington DC, Philadelphia, Atlanta and Detroit, the two acts played 48 shows in 64 days, selling out in practically every location. The Commodores' energetic and lively act – contrasting strongly with the more staid performance by the Philly trio – got rave reviews, with critics everywhere agreeing that the group had stolen the show from the headliners. Such reactions, according to one source close to the group, produced considerable rivalry between the O'Jays and The Commodores. Certainly the tour helped solidify the group's popularity so that by the time their fourth album, *Hot On The Tracks,* hit the record shops in June 1976, Motown had orders for half a million copies. The group were guaranteed a gold album.

Hot On The Tracks became The Commodores' first platinum album. Within months of release, it amassed sales of a million copies as a result of the song 'Just To Be Close To You' (which spent over three months on the US pop charts, making it to No.7 in *Billboard* on 9 October 1976 and giving the group another gold single). The era of Richie-penned hits had begun in earnest and was to continue right up until Lionel's departure from the group in 1982, with each new hit topping its predecessor.

'Just To Be Close To You' was something of a risk for the group, as Lionel noted: "Using that particular kind of slurred vocal style for the rap part of the tune – which took up a good portion of the song itself – was a gamble and, lucky for us, it was one that paid off." Here was Lionel's philosophy: "I feel that there are two kinds of entertainers, just like there are two kinds of people: those who play it safe and those who take risks, the gamblers. I see The Commodores as gamblers; if we win, we win big and people will say we're unique, we're trendsetters. If we fail, we'll just fade away. We had a relatively safe beginning with 'Machine Gun' but we've been in the business a while now so we're up against the real 'heavies'. The competition now is so stiff that we'd better take some risks and stay original. The Commodores haven't yet reached the status of, say, a Stevie Wonder. He could sneeze on a record and start a whole new trend!"

Lionel's attitude to songwriting becomes apparent in his remarks on 'Just To Be Close To You', which he wants ". . .the average 'Joes' to relate to. I knew the rap would appeal to people only if I did it the way folks actually spoke. I've heard raps where people tend to speak in perfect English, almost like film stars reading lines. But your average guy in the street doesn't talk like that, so I did the slurring and the stuttering which made the record so different from what you'd expect. And that's where I'm coming from with all the songs that I write. If I'm going to be a songwriter whose songs last, I'd better write lyrics that everyday people can relate to."

Hot On The Tracks featured four songs by Lionel, more than he'd had on any previous album. A democratic process of selecting material was intended to prevent any one member from mono- polizing an album with their own songs. "There are six writers, six producers, six arrangers and six musicians in this group, so it's tough because everyone has material they want to record with the group." The group would set aside a full day in Tuskegee – still home for all the members of the group at that time – to go over material they had prepared for each album. Occasionally, the selec- tion of material would stretch into two days. They collaborated on some songs together, using their own studio in Tuskegee for putting down demos and later, after final selections had been made, for rehearsals.

To avoid any serious confrontation between members of the group, James Carmichael's choice was final. "We'd even try sometimes to sneak material to Carmichael before the meeting – that's how competitive we were about it! We all wanted to get our songs on the album because naturally we felt ours were the best!" Ironically, it was this

40

The Commodores display their first platinum album and second gold album in a row, Hot On The Tracks, *during a visit to New York. Back row from left: Ronald LaPread, Milan Williams, Barney Ales, president of Motown Records, Thomas McClary and Benny Ashburn. Front row: Lionel, William King and Walter "Clyde" Orange.*

41

From left: Ronald LaPread, Lionel, William King, Thomas McClary, Walter "Clyde" Orange and Milan Williams.

method of song selection which was later to prove a determining factor in Lionel's decision to go solo. Lionel had become very prolific as a writer – "a fountain of creativity" – and it was obvious that he would never be able to use such a wealth of material, "which really expressed what I wanted to say musically," on Commodore albums.

The material submitted for selection invariably reflected each member's personal musical taste. Lionel emerged as the balladeer, even though his collaborations with Tommy McClary were usually funkier and more uptempo. Carmichael, using his extensive musical experience – with Cal Harris (and his assistant engineer Jane Clark) at the board – was frequently able to turn very rough material into a masterpiece. "They were willing to take risks and be inventive," recalls one of the production assistants who frequently attended The Commodores' recording sessions. "We'd start out doing the rhythm and we'd keep going until Carmichael really had the feeling that he wanted fully captured. Then the guys would individually clean up the tracks. Usually, after that, we'd add on the synthesizers and backgrounds before putting on the final leads. Then James would put together composites of maybe two or three different takes to come up with the final finished track."

Since Carmichael was "a perfectionist", the process frequently took a while – "but James never let anything out that he didn't feel fully represented him and the guys. What was so great at those sessions was the way he and the guys related. James has a very pleasant disposition but, at the same time, he knows what it takes to get the job done. You can imagine what it was like with six different personalities to contend with!"

The group took the whole recording process very seriously, operating a system of heavy fines for anyone who was late. This system had been imposed, when the group first began making an impact on the music scene, by manager Benny Ashburn who knew the importance of the group maintaining a businesslike attitude. It was particularly important that they should maintain that attitude now, for The Commodores were busier than ever; and with the success of 'Fancy Dancer'

there was to be no let up. 'Fancy Dancer', a mid-tempo, funk-oriented groove item which Lionel co-wrote with Ronnie LaPread, didn't hit pop audiences in quite the same way that 'Just To Be Close To You' – the ballad with its romantic, sensual feel – had. The song was a throwback to the sound that fans had come to associate with the group's first three albums. The fourth album, *Hot On The Tracks,* had reflected a slight change in the overall sound of the group, with a more prominent use of strings and the addition of synthesizer programming by Cal Harris, regarded by The Commodores as one of the people most responsible for the distinctive sound of their records. "Cal's what you might call 'an experimental engineer' – he tries anything and he gets a big kick out of some of the ideas we present to him."

William King defends the group's decision to release 'Dancer' as a follow-up to the group's biggest pop hit to date. "We didn't mind that the record didn't get quite the same kind of attention from pop audiences because we wanted to keep our r&b following. After all, they were our roots and our base and we didn't want to lose them or have them think that we'd 'sold out'. Plus we needed to have some funk in there to even things out, what with 'Sweet Love' and 'Just To Be Close', both ballads, now our biggest hit records."

At the end of 1976, Benny Ashburn was planning The Commodores' first European tour and the group's third visit to the Far East, where they had consolidated their previous success by winning a Bronze award at the Tokyo Music Festival earlier in the year. By the time their fifth album, *Commodores,* (their second platinum album), was released in March 1977, The Commodores were winging their way across the Atlantic in anticipation of a warm reception from British and European audiences.

Their first British dates – Birmingham, London, Leeds and Manchester – received critical acclaim. Sharon Davis wrote a vivid account of the group's first UK performance in *Blues and Soul.* "The Commodores put on one of the finest shows I've seen this year. . .the visual excitement never really lets up – spraying confetti, dense smoke, flashing

The Commodores and The Mean Machine take on the Penthouse Power baseball team.

46

lights, bangs, gun fires – believe me, this was no ordinary gig. Apart from the guys themselves, there were three back-ups of guitar, trumpet and sax who added vocal support. [Known as 'The Mean Machine', Darrell Jones, Harold Hudson and Gary Johnson – later replaced by Winston Sims – eventually expanded to four members with the addition of David Cochrane.] The more popular parts of their repertoire like 'Fancy Dancer', the mellow 'This Is Your Life', the smooth 'Just To Be Close To You' (which prompted well-deserved applause), 'High On Sunshine' and, my all-time favourite, 'Sweet Love', all drew great response and then 'Machine Gun' saw the entire audience out of their seats and dancing. The group wanted a party and, by the looks of things, they were getting exactly that! 'I Feel Sanctified' kept the pace going, at the end of which the group left the stage. The audience wasn't having that and demanded more.

"Back they came for a foot-stomping, hand-clapping, body-shaking 'Slippery When Wet'. It seemed that nothing could go wrong. The repertoire was well chosen for a balanced act; the choreography, when used on occasion, was brilliant and each group member appeared thoroughly happy. Somehow, this feeling that the group were exhibiting on stage swept around the theatre."

Unfortunately, the world tour was cut short at this point by the sudden death from cancer of Ronald LaPread's wife, Kathy Faye. The group did just one show without Ronnie before deciding to abandon the rest of the tour, and they returned home at the end of March. It was a demonstration of the close family feeling that the group shared both on and off stage; back then, with each step bringing the group further recognition, there was never a thought that anyone would consider going it alone. Lionel, however, was contributing more and more to the group's success. He was no longer just the group's singer who still occasionally played sax on most of the songs: he also provided the group with the songs that were taking them into a whole new league.

Lionel with Thomas McClary.

On tour, The Commodores put on a spectacular and exciting show, drawing capacity crowds everywhere.

From left: Walter King, Lionel Richie, Thomas McClary, Ronald LaPread, Milan Williams, Walter "Clyde" Orange, Benny Ashburn.

54

By 1977, The Commodores had become the most popular black act in the United States, second only to Earth, Wind & Fire in their ability to draw capacity crowds and put on a spectacular, energetic and exciting show. EW&F shows tended to be a little more adventurous – Verdine White, the group's bassist, would levitate, spaceships descended, and members of the group seemingly vanished into thin air. Given the more inspirational nature of leader Maurice White's lyrics ('Slippery When Wet', 'I Feel Sanctified' or 'Fancy Dancer' were not exactly 'Devotion', 'That's The Way Of The World' and 'All About Love'), the audience reaction to the two groups was markedly different. While EW&F's very mixed crowd lit matches as Philip Bailey sang 'Reasons', The Commodores' mostly black audience would be partying to the sounds of 'Machine Gun'.

In the US, records by black artists usually had to make it on the r&b charts before being played on pop radio stations. 'Easy', a million-seller, became the first Commodores' record to go straight into the pop charts (ending up at No. 4 on 25 June). In July 1977, the song also became the group's biggest British hit; it reached No.9 on the charts, eclipsing the group's previous British hits, 'Machine Gun' and 'The Zoo'.

'Easy', which US columnist Nelson George described in a retrospective on Lionel and the group in 1983 as "a wonderfully realised Southern landscape in sound", became Richie's first pop standard and, as such, led to inevitable comments about his intentions.

The Commodores' success with this simple ballad came at a time when the music world was overrun by the sound of disco. Disco had begun life back in 1973 and 1974 with classics like Gloria Gaynor's version of The Jacksons' 'Never Can Say Goodbye', George McRae's 'Rock Your Baby' and The Hues Corporation's 'Rock The Boat'. By 1976, the music had produced its own heroes – Donna Summer, K.C. and The Sunshine Band, The Trammps and others – and it arrived in full force that year with the epic *Saturday Night Fever,* a tribute on celluloid and vinyl to the lifestyles of thousands of teenagers across the globe.

Recording artists – both black and white – who'd been around for a while, were given little option: either record disco music or don't bother to record at all. Singers like Motown's Thelma Houston, with her rendition of 'Don't Leave Me This Way', and Esther Phillips, with her version of the standard 'What A Difference A Day Makes', complied, ending up with the biggest hits of their careers. With disco dominating the music scene, The Commodores (who had made their own contribution to the beginnings of the movement with 'Machine Gun') were, as Lionel put it, "willing to take risks" by putting out a song like 'Easy'. The sound of The Commodores was never the same after that record.

'Easy', moreover, marked the time when Lionel started to become the identifiable "face" of The Commodores and, increasingly, the group's official spokesman. Until then, drummer Walter "Clyde" Orange frequently shared the duties of "lead singer", even though it was Lionel who was frequently singled out by critics for his vocal prowess. Lionel had been the centre of attention on stage as early as 1975 – even before his ballads made such an impact on the group's success. As *Variety* pointed out in their review of The Commodores' show at New York's Felt Forum in September '75 – when they were second-billed to Graham Central Station – "Lionel Richie is strongly featured."

The absence of any recognizable personality for the group was a strange phenomenon in itself. Mick Jagger was always identified as The Rolling Stones' leader and Michael was clearly the centre of attention in The Jacksons long before he became a solo artist. Neither The Commodores nor Earth, Wind & Fire, by now the two dominant black groups on the music scene, had any one prominent member – even though Lionel sang the majority of The Commodores' leads and Philip Bailey and Maurice White shared the same function for EW&F.

Still very much a close-knit group, The Commodores were busy capitalising on their new level of acceptance and coping with their inevitably hectic schedule. A typical day in the life of the group on the road was described by *Billboard* in 1977 as "getting up at 6.30, having breakfast at 7.30, getting on the bus at 8.30, arriving at the location for the show at 1.30, soundcheck from 4.30 for several hours, dinner and then on stage at 10.00 and back in bed by 2.00 if you're lucky!" Lionel reflected that "although lots of groups relax when they have free time, we work constantly." When The Commodores did find time to relax they would "play tennis, fly and go out boating" – usually together. And on the increasingly rare times they were at home, the group would communicate with each other via CB radio. Everyone had a code name: Lionel was "Skeet", Ronald "Shaggy Dog", Milan "Captain Quick-draw", William "WAK", Thomas "Adam Ant", and Walter "Sweet Clyde".

The group seemed to spend almost every waking hour together; this was bound to produce its share of tensions, though the official party line was always: "We're one happy family." The Commodores were fortunate in having Benny Ashburn as their mentor and manager; he could always be counted on to "smooth out any differences and really be like a father to the group."

Ashburn was there to ensure that no internal disagreements surfaced in public and that the group's image remained untarnished. He instituted a fines system whereby any group member found taking drugs could be fined as much as $1,000 a time. He also maintained a veil of privacy over The Commodores' private lives. For many years, no mention was made of the group's marital status even though Gwen Williams, Ann Orange, Shirley King, Brenda Richie and Kathy LaPread had provided their husbands with a great deal of moral and emotional support when The Commodores were working almost non-stop. Ashburn felt that any such revelation might well alienate their female fans.

In August 1977, the group recommenced the world tour they had called off in March when Ronald LaPread's wife had died. The tour lasted through to May 1978, and most of that time was spent in Europe. The first big leg of the tour, however, was domestic; the group played at major

58

Back row from left: Thomas McClary, Ronald LaPread, Lionel. Front row: Walter "Clyde" Orange, William King and Milan Williams.

Back row from left: Thomas McClary, Lionel, Ronald LaPread, William King and Walter "Clyde" Orange. Front row: Milan Williams and Stephanie Mills.

venues throughout the United States to upwards of 10,000 people. A typical show featured 12 songs and lasted 80 minutes. The Commodores' stage outfits (which weighed several pounds each) were invariably heavily-sequined and incorporated some type of military design – either shoulder-pads or breast-plates – in keeping with the group's naval name.

The tour coincided with the release of another single, 'Brick House', a slab of Commodore-style funk written by all six members of the group. Although it was a "straight r&b record", The Commodores' acceptance on the playlists of pop radio stations propelled 'Brick House' to the No.5 spot on the pop charts in September. The *Commodores* album became a platinum seller. The album was something of a landmark for the group; it had yielded two gold singles with 'Brick House' and 'Easy', and it had given the group another run of

success overseas. In the UK, the LP was known as *Zoom* and the title track, a Richie-LaPread composition, was released as a single in this country only – providing the group with another British hit (it reached No.32 on the charts when released in September 1977).

The Commodores continued to pick up accolades and awards for their work. They won the NAACP Image Award in 1976 and in 1977; they were named Top Group in Brazil in 1977; and they were given a special award by Tuskegee Institute. In 1977 the American music magazine *Cashbox* named The Commodores the "Best Group Of The Year". They had become, in the words of one writer, "the best party band in pop. . .the black equivalent of Journey or REO Speedwagon." It looked as if nothing could stop The Commodores from becoming giants in the music business.

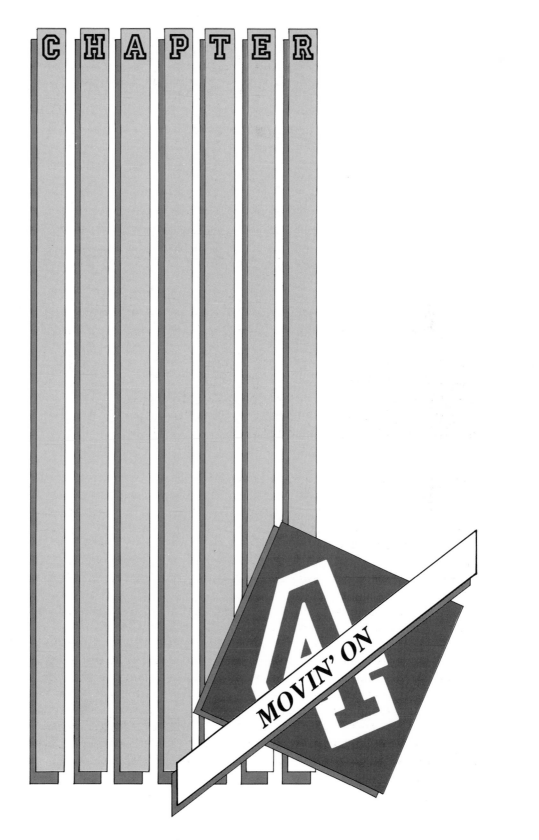

CHAPTER

MOVIN' ON

4

With record sales in the millions and sell-out concerts now the norm, The Commodores were ready to move into new areas of the entertainment industry. The film *Thank God It's Friday* – a joint production by the film divisions of Motown and Casablanca Records – gave the group their first chance to do just that. Released in June 1978, the movie starred Donna Summer as an aspiring singer who finds stardom after conning her way into a disco where The Commodores are appearing, and begging for the chance to sing. The movie, described by one critic as "about as monotonous and uninventive as disco music itself," ended up as one of the top grossing films of the year. It won an Oscar for Donna Summer's 'Last Dance' hit, just one of some 32 songs included in the soundtrack. One of the songs featured was The Commodores' 'Too Hot Ta Trot', which came out in November 1977 (the original release date for the movie). By the time the film was shown, the record had already given The Commodores a Top 10 hit in the US.

A "live" double album also came out in October '77 – giving the group a platinum album in both the US and in Holland – though Lionel was less than satisfied with it: ". . .we understand Motown's desire to cut all of the rapping we do between numbers, but it's an integral part of the show and it makes it look as though all we did was a 'live' album in the studio whereas the idea was to capture our 'live' show on record. By missing out the little gestures in our regular show, our act appears disjointed on the record." Lionel hinted in an interview he gave in April 1977 that The Commodores' relationship with Motown had had its share of ups and downs: "It's been a learning process for us and Motown, a gradual process throughout the past few years. We've had to learn how each other works and occasionally things happen that we don't agree with – like the sleeve designs on some of our albums which haven't featured us on the front. But we're getting more into having control over different aspects of our career, so I'm not complaining. In fact, Motown's the place we'd like to be for the rest of our career."

*Lionel accepts a special award
from Motown for over half a
million sales of 'Three Times
A Lady' in the UK.*

Lionel's confidence in the company was clearly high as he and The Commodores – through the management division of their burgeoning Commodores Entertainment Corporation (CEC) – signed two acts to Motown. One, The Three Ounces Of Love, a female group from Detroit, frequently opened shows for The Commodores in 1978 and 1979; the other, Platinum Hook, was a self-contained soul and funk group. The Commodores hired Motown staff producers, like Michael Sutton, to work with the acts. Unfortunately, neither act received the kind of attention likely to bring them hit status and eventually they were both dropped from the company's roster.

CEC, the partnership formed by The Commodores and Benny Ashburn at the start of their business relationship, had grown over the years; by 1978, the company had seven working divisions and a staff of eight. The management division, with a total of ten acts signed to its roster (including The Mean Machine and producer James Carmichael), had been formed so that the group could share the knowledge they had gained in the music business with young artists who were just starting out. Similarly, the publishing division, with five outside songwriters under contract, was intended to develop young talent; it also handled all of The Commodores' songs.

The company's other activities included a transportation arm, known as "The Commodores Moving On Company", which owned three buses, two tractor trailers, seven Mercedes-Benz and two limos; when not in use by The Commodores, they were available for hire to other acts. There was also a tour division for The Commodores' road, sound and lights crews; a licensing division for Commodores' T-shirts, belt-buckles, decals and posters; a fan club with over 5,000 members; and a sponsorship division for the group's work with companies like Schlitz Beer (they started doing commercials for Schlitz in 1978). CEC also managed the group's investments in African art and rare coins, and in real estate (they owned "The Studio", a rehearsal hall/recording studio complex in Tuskegee, as well as property in Los Angeles, Houston and Alabama).

Beginning in 1976, the group's schedule called for two albums, as well as domestic and international tours, each year. The Commodores had become one of the busiest black acts in the business. By mid-1978, they eclipsed all previous achievements with another Richie-written song that took the group to No.1 on all charts. 'Three Times A Lady' spent two weeks at the top of the US Hot Hundred in July, and it achieved the same status in the UK in August. The record earned The Commodores a double platinum award (two million sales) at home, and gold records in the UK – where it became one of Motown's biggest-selling singles (with sales of over 950,000) – and Australia. The song also gave The Commodores the distinction of earning an ASCAP Country Songs Award, so universal was its appeal.

Lionel relates the story behind 'Three Times A Lady': "I attended the wedding anniversary of my parents, and my father made a speech about how much he loved my mother and appreciated the way she had stood beside him for thirty-seven years. I started to think about my own life and how my wife stands by me, how she does so many beautiful things without being asked. So I wrote the song as a dedication to my wife and my mother. I got some idea of people's reaction to it when my next-door neighbour said that if a man wanted to buy her a present, all he need do is buy her that record and he wouldn't have to say anything else. From the masses of awards the song has won, it seems that the whole world really does love that song. I think it's every songwriter's dream to be totally accepted and, I've got to say, it's a great feeling."

William King remembers the first time Lionel presented the song to the group: "He didn't have all the lyrics together when he first brought it to us. But we knew right off the bat that the song was a smash, so we constructed the album in such a way that the other songs would lead up to and around 'Three Times A Lady'." The song's success resulted in sales in excess of three million copies for the *Natural High* album, earning the group their first triple platinum album.

The record also resulted in the group extending the domestic half of their world tour (which had begun the previous autumn in 1977). "We ended up doing 108 dates in all, instead of the 68 we had

originally planned. As the record kept selling, so more and more dates were added. With the acceptance in the country and western market, we were playing places we hadn't played before." By the time The Commodores started the international leg of their tour, 'Three Times A Lady' had hit the charts throughout Europe, South America and the Far East. Starting in April, the itinerary included stops in the UK (Bristol, Birmingham, Edinburgh, Glasgow, Manchester and London), Belgium, The Netherlands, Germany and Switzerland; wherever The Commodores went, they played to packed houses. They returned home to find that 'Three Times A Lady' had been recorded by a variety of

musicians, including Johnny Mathis, Nate Harvell, the country singer, and Andre Kostelantz. Kostelantz recorded a classical version with the Philharmonic Orchestra – "a true honour" Lionel commented. "Having one of my songs done by such an illustrious musician was real important for me." The record, according to Thomas McClary, "finally made people stop categorising us and start appreciating us for our music."

The group ended 1978 with the release of a *Greatest Hits* album, containing all their hit singles from 'Machine Gun' through to 'Easy'. It garnered a platinum album for them at home, and provided them with their first gold LP awards in the UK

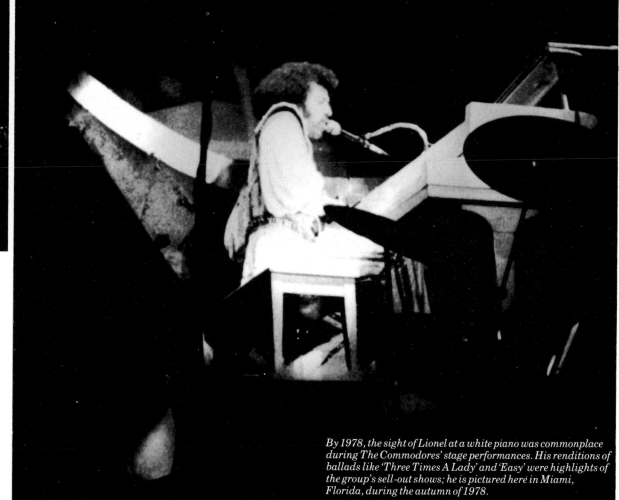

By 1978, the sight of Lionel at a white piano was commonplace during The Commodores' stage performances. His renditions of ballads like 'Three Times A Lady' and 'Easy' were highlights of the group's sell-out shows; he is pictured here in Miami, Florida, during the autumn of 1978.

(where the album was compiled differently) and in New Zealand. The Commodores also received a top box-office award for acts who played at arenas with between 6,000 and 20,000 people. The non-stop touring, however, was beginning to take its toll. The Commodores had begun a national 90-day US tour on 29 June (it ended on 23 November) almost immediately after returning from Europe at the end of May. Benny Ashburn responded to comments by admitting that "the group has been going through some emotional trips because of the length of the last two tours."

A review of The Commodores' New York appearance in July noted that the group had failed to sell out Madison Square Garden, as they had done in October 1977, "with just three-quarters of the stadium full." Critics suggested that the soul/funk group LTD, who opened for The Commodores, had been stealing the limelight. In some cases, audiences left after hearing LTD's set. "LTD are more of a boogeying band," Ashburn explained. "Because of the hits we've had with our ballads, we now do five slow numbers in the show. People used to think of us as strictly a high energy band so there is some readjustment." There were "problems" he noted, "with getting some of our black audiences back. After 'Three Times A Lady', we definitely lost some of our black base and we started playing places where our audiences were eighty per cent white."

The group, Ashburn stated, "would only do an international tour in 1979 – we'll also do a sound-track and a television special – we won't be touring the US next year." The Commodores may not have gone out on the road in the US during 1979, but it didn't affect the group's success on record – and, once again, it was Lionel's songs that were responsible.

Their album, *Midnight Magic* – another triple platinum seller – was released in July, a few weeks after the first single from the LP had hit the streets. 'Sail On', with its memorable melody, became an immediate chart topper, reaching the No.4 position on the US Hot Hundred and No.8 on the British charts. Lionel remembers how the song ended up on the *Midnight Magic* album: "I wrote a country song but it wasn't really meant for The Commodores – I just felt 'country' that day – it was more like a joke,

me writing this country and western song. As usual, I logged it and put it in my files. Well, our producer James Carmichael came by my house. He asked me if I had any songs for the new LP and I said, 'Do you want to hear something crazy?' and I played him this country song. He said 'Richie, that's it. Throw out whatever else you've got!' And that's how 'Sail On' came to be recorded."

It seemed as if every new record was being snapped up by pop fans everywhere. The Commodores were now known as the "crossover killers", a term used to describe black artists who succeeded in capturing pop audiences as well as keeping their r&b base; and, inevitably, some of The Commodores' original fans felt they had "sold out".

William King summed up the group's position in July 1979, just a month before The Commodores arrived in the UK on the first leg of their world tour: "In the last two years, we've made more money from performances than any black group has ever done before. Our plan has always been to surpass The Beatles; they came as close as anybody has ever done to reaching everyone but they missed out on a couple of things, purely by timing. For example, the r&b crowd would never touch them – even if they liked them! They came during an era of conflict between black and white. You didn't see any Beatles' records on the floor of an average black home, like you might to some extent see that now with The Bee Gees. Times have changed. Now it doesn't matter much what colour you are. When we did a tour of the Midwest, eighty per cent of the audiences were white. We did a show in Seattle, Washington, that was ninety-nine per cent white. The world is getting better; it may not always look like it, but it is improving."

The group's world tour encompassed Europe (including stops in Paris, Brussels, Munich, Stockholm, Oslo and Amsterdam), Asia and South America. On their 1977 tour, The Commodores had played at houses holding a maximum of 2,500 people. On this occasion, the group played two nights at the Wembley Arena, and in Glasgow and Stafford at venues with a capacity for between 8,000 and 10,000 fans. The Emotions, who'd enjoyed a big international hit with 'The Best Of My Love' in 1978, opened for the group. The Commodores' act included 'Easy', 'Flying High', 'Brick House', 'Zoom', and 'Too Hot Ta Trot'; but it was the Richie ballads – 'Three Times A Lady', 'Still' and 'Sail On' – which elicited the strongest response.

Reviewer Gof Abbey wrote in his commentary on the Wembley concert in a September issue of *Blues & Soul*: "Out of the bank of speakers booms the voice of Lionel Richie who sets about convincing the audience, as if they need convincing, just how grateful the group were to them for making 'Three Times A Lady' a number one hit last year. Just as he begins to wind up his speech, a white piano is raised behind the drum kits, with Mr Richie suitably seated to begin the intro to 'Still'. . .as the dry ice receded,

the song came to an end and the roof was almost raised from the rafters by the deafening applause. As if that wasn't enough to bring the house down, Richie calmly announced that the next song was dedicated to everyone there and began the piano opening to 'Three Times A Lady'."

In 1979, in another interview with *Blues & Soul*, talk surfaced of the possibility of solo albums by members of the group. William King suggested: "It's not out of the picture. Individually, some of the guys are very talented and, if they should want to do a solo thing, they shouldn't be hindered." He went on: "Right now, though, the group needs to be a group. The Commodores don't plan to end up like The Beatles – breaking up something great that's been working. All of our effort and time should be put into the group. But, in time, who knows? For example, "Clyde" has such a good voice. Everyone associates Richie's voice with the group and "Clyde" has never been able to maintain himself as a singer. And we all feel he should. . .it was his voice on 'Brick House' by the way."

Although the group were anxious to maintain the official status quo – a democratic situation in which no one member of the group was singled out as more talented or creative than any other – it was clear who would be the first in line to do a solo album. "In time, I think a solo LP is inevitable," was Lionel's comment, although in 1981 he noted: "I've been solo for thirteen years. I was solo in The Commodores and now I'm getting solo outside the group but I'm still in The Commodores. What really constitutes going solo for me is going on stage with a brand-new drummer, a new bass player, a guitar player and a new keyboard player. I already have the best. . .we've been together for thirteen years."

Things were going well for the group and making any shift at that time would have made no sense. They had done a very successful commercial for Schlitz beer, were considering doing a full-length movie, were writing the theme song for a movie, "Underground Aces", working on a television special (shown at Christmas 1980, featuring the group with The Pointer Sisters as special guests), and they were even being asked to play at private parties across the globe – an oil sheik reportedly paid

From left: Lionel, Milan Williams, William King, Ronald LaPread, Thomas McClary and Walter "Clyde" Orange.

Lionel, Kenny Rogers and William King.

them a small fortune to play at his daughter's wedding party in Switzerland. The group ended the year with yet another Richie smash, 'Still'; released in September 1979, it topped the US charts the following month and made the British Top 5 in November. The song, later recorded by Mantovani and Wayne Newton, completed a run of Richie songs which had taken the group to the upper reaches of the charts. Four of those songs, 'Brick House', 'Easy', 'Three Times A Lady' and 'Sail On', had earned Grammy nominations for Lionel and The Commodores – although Earth, Wind and Fire had pipped the group to the post on almost every single occasion. However, industry recognition didn't affect the group's standing with Motown. In 1979, the group re-signed with Motown for another seven years. They signed a multi-million dollar contract, stipulating the release of an album every nine months. It looked as if nothing could stop The Commodores from becoming the hottest group in the country.

1980 brought a new chapter in the story, however. It was the first year the group failed to have their usual run of Top 10 hits; 'Old Fashioned Love' only just made the Top 20 when it was released in July. It was also the first year that Lionel started working on outside projects, making him the second member of the group to do so (Ronald LaPread had produced the r&b group Seventh Wonder for Casablanca Records without any notable success in 1979).

Pop-country star Kenny Rogers was very impressed with the material Lionel had been writing, and he wanted Lionel to write a song for him. It was June, and The Commodores were about to begin a 96-day tour scheduled to end on December 7. (They had just returned from a tour of the Far East – where they performed as headliners at the Tokyo Music Festival – Australia, New Zealand, Hawaii and South America.) Lionel recalls: "Two weeks before our tour started his office called with the request. I had to turn it down to start with because I didn't think I'd have time, what with getting ready to go out on the road.

"Well, as fate would have it, 'Clyde' Orange was riding on his motorcycle and fell off. We had to postpone going out on tour until he was fully recovered, which took some three weeks. So I called Kenny's office back and asked them if they were still interested and, that same night, I was in Las Vegas playing him the song 'Lady'. That song had originally been planned for The Commodores and giving it up was hard. But it was like Paul Anka when he gave the song 'My Way' to Frank Sinatra. He knew it would open him up to a much wider audience; that's exactly what happened for him and that's what happened for me too. The union with Kenny was well worth it."

Describing their working relationship, Lionel had this to say: "He's so genuine. He just rolled up his sleeves when it was time to get to work and said:

"Whatever it takes to get what you want from me, just let me know." I produced Kenny literally standing side by side with him in the booth in the studio. To do just two songs ['Lady' and 'Goin' Back To Alabama'] he spent eight and a half hours in that booth and never really took a break. We got them done in that one night using just four rhythm musicians and a few string and horn players and he did a heck of a job on them." That night in the studio with Kenny turned out to be the start of a whole new era in Lionel's career, something he couldn't have known at the time.

After that first Rogers' session, The Commodores hit the road for their first big tour since 1978. This tour was arranged a little differently from previous tours, as William King explained: "We're generally working four days, Thursdays through Sundays, and that gives us the rest of the week to go home or do whatever we want. Not only that, but we're actually travelling by bus a lot more, since the dates are being grouped together geographically. I feel that this is the best show we have ever put on. The excitement is there on stage and we have come up with some fabulous stage effects. The people who did The Bee Gees last big tour staged this one with us and we ended up using something like 360 lights. At first, we had more lights but it just got too hot – it was like a pressure-cooker out there! And the stage costumes are the best we've ever had."

One of the highlights of the tour was the group's appearance at Madison Square Garden in New York, but the event was marred by vandals who ran amok before and after the show, attacking innocent bystanders and stealing jewellery. The New York press picked up the story and, for a time, many people thought it was The Commodores' music which had incited the hooligans. The group went to great pains to deny this; indeed it was difficult to see what could have aroused such havoc, particularly since the show ended with 'Jesus Is Love', a gospel track from the *Heroes* LP released in June 1980, complete with a full choir hired especially for the occasion.

Lionel talked about this song in an interview he gave in January 1981: "I didn't sit down to write a gospel song *per se*. I guess it was because of my

frustration from listening to the news every night. We've cluttered up our lives with money, wars and so on, and I just felt my inner frustration come out. And then I was in conflict with myself as to whether I should use certain words. Should I use 'Jesus'? Should I use 'He'? Then I said, 'Wait a minute, the full value of the song is its reference to Jesus, so let me give it that full value.'" Lionel's earlier inclination to be a preacher appeared to be surfacing in his music.

However, the majority of the group's fans were not impressed, and the album *Heroes* failed to spark any great excitement either, though it was nominated for a Grammy in 1980. The title track, a Richie composition, focused on the message that "everyone is a hero" – but the fact that the album didn't contain the traditional Commodore ballads definitely hindered its acceptance. Aside from 'Jesus Is Love' the album contained another gospel-oriented song, 'Mighty Spirit' (written by William King). Critics claimed the album was "self-indulgent". Lionel's response was straightforward: "Sure, we were disappointed about it, but we weren't really surprised. When we left our standard ballad off the album, we knew we were getting a little risky. We took a gamble and realised we were sacrificing airplay by putting a song like 'Jesus Is Love' on there. But all of a sudden, we started getting hundreds of letters concerning religion, so it isn't all about a hit record anymore."

Lionel went on to discuss the shift in the way the group projected itself; previously, they had presented an anonymous front. "Now it's about personalities. The fans want to be able to relate to people in the group. Hit records are one thing but they are a year-by-year phenomena. . .personalities last for ever." What was becoming patently clear was that it was Lionel who was developing his public image quite considerably, aided by a few fortunate developments in his involvement with projects outside The Commodores.

Lionel's initial work with Kenny Rogers had been very successful; 'Lady', written and produced by Lionel, retained the No.1 spot on the pop charts for a total of six weeks in September and October 1980, and it earned Lionel two Grammy nominations. The song was also featured on Rogers' *Greatest Hits*

album, released in 1981, which sold an astounding 15 million copies. Anxious to repeat their successful collaboration, Lionel and Kenny went back into the recording studios in the spring of 1981 to record a whole album. Entitled *Share Your Love With Me* (an old hit for blues singer Bobby Bland), the set included several Richie compositions, including the highly successful 'I Don't Need You', which made it to No.3 on the pop charts in June 1981. Lionel said that although he'd tailored specific songs like 'The Good Life' for Kenny, "everything I write could be for The Commodores!" Nevertheless, Lionel knew perfectly well that working with Rogers was an excellent opportunity to develop his burgeoning talents as a producer.

Working with Rogers in 1980 had brought Lionel into contact with the singer's manager, Ken Kragen, for the first time. Kragen, who'd received an MBA at Harvard in Business Studies, had been managing pop and country acts – such as The Limelighters, The Smothers Brothers and Glenn Yarborough – for nearly fifteen years when he formed Ken Kragen & Co. in 1979. He acquired Rogers and country singer Dottie West as clients, later adding pop singers Jennifer Warnes and Kim Carnes to the roster. Married to former actress Cathy Worthington, Kragen had built a formidable reputation for himself as an effective negotiator. With his work as a producer of television specials (he produced Rogers' television movie *The Gambler* for CBS) he further expanded his company's activities. Rumours began to circulate in the US music press that Lionel would hire Kragen to manage him as a solo act, while still continuing his association with Benny Ashburn for his work with The Commodores. Ashburn stated emphatically that such an eventuality was "impossible", although developments in Lionel's career in the coming months affected his business situation significantly.

Working on the *Share Your Love* album with Kenny Rogers also afforded Lionel his first opportunity to use the talents of his wife, Brenda. Since their marriage in 1975, Brenda had spent most of her time at home in Tuskegee, although she'd begun to travel on the road with Lionel whenever she could. "It's strange because I was looking for a production assistant and I hadn't realised that for seven years, since we'd gotten married, Brenda had been peeping over my shoulder and watching people at Motown like Suzee Ikeda, Suzanne De Passe and James Carmichael. I thought she was playing when she'd come to the studio with us, but she was studying all the time, and she said she'd like to be my production assistant.

"I had some real heavy production commitments coming up and I didn't want to use it as a learning period for her – but she insisted! So I agreed that she could give it a try on Kenny's album – she was so organised and so on top of things that she scared me. Not only did she do what a production assistant is supposed to do – she also organised my whole day, who I should see, who I should not see, and those I didn't have time to see she would meet on my behalf. She even organised my food!"

At the same time as working on the Kenny Rogers album, Lionel was also recording the title track for the movie *Endless Love*, starring Brooke Shields. Polygram Records had originally asked Lionel to compose an instrumental for the soundtrack. "They said they wanted a 'Love Story' type of song," Lionel commented. "Then the film's director, Franco Zeffirelli – someone I really admire for his sensitivity – asked me to write some lyrics. So I came up with them, little knowing that they were going to ask me to sing them too! This was all in between doing sessions for Kenny's album and The Commodores' *In The Pocket* album, so I was trying to figure out how to fit it all in. Then came the icing on the cake: I got the call telling me that Franco and Polygram had a certain Ms Ross to sing with me! The funny thing was that three months before that I'd seen Diana out in California on a vacation and we'd talked about how nice it would be to do a duet someday. Someday came quicker than I'd ever imagined it would."

Lionel was presented with an interesting logistical problem. Diana had just completed performing for several nights in Atlantic City, New Jersey, and her next dates were in Lake Tahoe, Nevada. Lionel, meanwhile, was busy recording with Kenny and The Commodores in Los Angeles. So, to get the movie theme cut, Diana and Lionel recorded in Reno, Nevada, "in a studio smaller than my bathroom!"

(Lionel apparently wrote quite a number of his hit songs in his bathroom at home – "it's the only place I can go to get away from everyone and everything.")

Lionel's schedule was crazy. He'd record with The Commodores from noon to six and with Kenny Rogers from six to midnight; then he'd fly to Reno to meet with Ross, who had finished her last show in Tahoe – an hour's drive from Reno – at 1am. "The duet was completed by 4.30am and then we spent the next few hours just fooling around. We didn't leave until nine the next morning!"

No sooner had the vocals been done than Lionel started the mixing. "The routine now changes around a little – I'd start out with Kenny from 10am to 6pm, work on 'Endless Love' from 6pm to 9pm, then spend 9pm to 2am with The Commodores. It was pretty rough going for a while but thankfully Brenda was around. She'd have my breakfast ready, make sure I had a protein drink in the afternoon and then, at 6pm every night, we'd get our dinners in the studio."

All Lionel's hard work paid off handsomely. When 'Endless Love' was released in June 1981 it became a huge hit, holding the No.1 spot on the pop charts for nine weeks (and, as a result of the theme song, the movie attracted larger audiences). The record was on the British charts for a total of twelve weeks after its release in July, peaking at No.7 in September. It earned Lionel a total of five Grammy nominations, two awards from the American Music Association, the People's Choice Award, and the American Movie Award. The track turned out to be one of the company's biggest-selling singles ever, and Diana's swansong to Motown: she was just about to sign a deal with RCA in the US and with Capitol for the rest of the world.

But there was no Ross-Richie follow-up. "We thought about doing one, but the song couldn't really be followed," says Lionel. "But, boy, it was a great duet. Diana was a real professional and, when I think about the session, I can't help but laugh. At one point, Diana was singing her part and I was so mesmerised that I didn't realise she was through and there she was waiting for me to come in with my part. Then I thought – 'Oh my, Diana Ross, *the* Diana Ross is waiting on me!' It was a great experience, a once in a lifetime thing."

Interestingly, Ross recorded the song again in solo form for her RCA debut album, and the two worked together in 1984 when Lionel and James Carmichael produced Diana on the song 'Missing You'. It was a tribute to the late Marvin Gaye, which Lionel had written specifically for Diana, and it was included on her *Swept Away* album.

While Lionel was hitting the top of the charts with Ross, and collaborating successfully with Kenny Rogers, his work with The Commodores was suffering. Their *In The Pocket* album (the first Commodores' LP not to be recorded at Motown Studios – it was cut in Atlanta at Web IV Studios and in Hollywood at A&M's studios) was released in June 1981. It did moderately well, compared with the multi-million sales of the group's previous albums, though it spawned the hits 'Lady (You Bring Me Up)', which made it to No.8 on the charts in July, and 'Oh No', a Richie song which made it to the No.4 slot on the US Hot Hundred in October – essentially The Commodores' last big hit with its original line-up.

Although Lionel insisted that all was well in The Commodores' camp, in interviews with the press he seemed unsure as to where he was going. In answer to the question "Are you leaving the group?" Lionel shot back: "You've got to know I've had that question thrown at me so many times especially since 'Three Times A Lady'. Of course, no one knows what life will bring down the line but, right now, I'm having such a good time with those crazy guys – more fun than ever! And I'm not confined to just being a Commodore. I can do my outside work and then come back to the group when it's necessary. I believe I'm getting the best of both worlds; and by returning to the group each time I finish another outside project, I believe I can only enhance the group and our reputation. I don't think I need to put dynamite under the base of thirteen years of to-getherness in order to launch Lionel Richie. I feel a certain loyalty to these guys. So any ideas about blowing up the house to build another one aren't even there."

Lionel then confirmed that he was making plans "so fast you wouldn't believe for the first solo

One of the highlights of 1982 for Lionel was his appearance at the Oscar A ceremony in LA, where he performed 'Endless Love' with Diana Ross.

80

album! That will definitely be my next project." And, to add to the confusion, he added: "In terms of an all-out solo thing, I don't feel that will ever be necessary. I need to build Lionel Richie some more because I want to make sure the cushion is there. A lot of times a solo situation can fall flat on its face and there isn't always something to fall back on. Within the group, there's a lot of love and if I were to say tomorrow that I had to go solo, I'd need a new band, the whole thing. But I figure I've got the best in the business now, so why would I even think about that? Sure, as a group we're going through a period of growth, but it doesn't have to be a traumatic one. It's almost like a well-planned marriage. The idea is to get over the hurdles. After all, after every big argument the marriage gets better."

The other members of The Commodores never made public their feelings about Lionel's work outside the group. But someone who worked closely with them at that time suggests that there was some rivalry and resentment, if only because Lionel's work had eclipsed the group's efforts. Lionel had three different productions on the charts – Kenny Rogers' 'I Don't Need You', his duet with Diana Ross on 'Endless Love' and the group's 'Lady (You Bring Me Up)'. The question that hung heavy for The Commodores in the autumn of 1981 was not whether Lionel would go solo but when, and how it would affect the fortunes of the group.

Asked what his future plans were, Richie responded that some kind of "flashy answer is what I'm expected to give to that question. Truly, everything has happened so fast and things are taking off on such an outrageous level that I really don't know what I'm going to do next. It's one thing just having a hit record but it's something entirely different and somewhat devastating when a 'Three Times A Lady' happens. You have to change your life around – I mean, some people would retire after a song like that! But then when you have 'Sail On' and 'Still' and then 'Lady' and 'Endless Love', it's like, phew!"

Not everyone was thrilled with the way Lionel had been so completely embraced by pop audiences. Die-hard Commodore fans (who had supported the group's early hits like 'Machine Gun' and 'Slippery

When Wet') felt that Lionel and the group had foregone their r&b roots for the lusher pastures of more commercial music. Certainly, The Commodores were no longer seen as the epitome of funk. But with money rolling in from royalties on all the ballads he'd written, Lionel wasn't complaining. Rather, he was contemplating his next move and taking steps to capitalise on the success he was enjoying as a producer and songwriter.

So it came as no surprise when, in August, Lionel announced that he had signed with Ken Kragen's creative services division who would be advising him "on television and movie situations" and "moulding [his] public image." The writing was on the wall: now that his new business alliance with Kragen had begun, there was little question that Lionel was headed for a solo career without The Commodores.

CHAPTER

STEPPING OUT

When I'm really not sure what my next move should be, I go home to Tuskegee to the room on campus that I bought in 1978. It's the same room I used to occupy when I was in college, with all my old belongings in it. After I've spent some time in there by myself, I go to see my grandmother, Adelaide, and I listen to what she has to say." With work demanding that they spend more time in Los Angeles, the Richies had moved there – temporarily staying at Kenny Rogers' vast estate – even though they still maintained their home in Tuskegee. At the start of 1982, Lionel was in Tuskegee pondering what to do next. One thing was clear: a solo album had to be attempted.

Work began on the project that spring. Lionel decided to use the services of his old associate James Carmichael who had worked with The Commodores from the time of 'Machine Gun'. "He's been my trusted ear for years," was Lionel's comment. "He's been my backbone and I know I can count on him to steer me in the right direction. I remember when we first sat down to go over material for the solo album, I had over eighty unrecorded songs. He asked me to sort them into two piles – the songs I wanted to do and the songs I wanted other people to do – and then he told me that the pile of songs for others was the one we'd use to make our final selection for the album itself."

As it turned out, the album was more diversified than many critics had anticipated; a subtle balance had been created between the mid-tempo, r&b style of songs like 'Round And Round' and 'Serves You Right', and the ballads, 'Truly' and 'Wandering Stranger'. Lionel hired many of LA's top session musicians – Greg Phillinganes, who co-wrote 'Serves You Right' with Lionel and who played on Michael Jackson's *Off The Wall* and *Thriller* albums, Nathan Watts, Paul Jackson, Paulinho da Costa, Michael Bodikker, Ndugu Chancler and Clarence MacDonald. Guitarist Joe Walsh, tennis star Jimmy Connors (who made his musical debut singing background on 'Tell Me') and Kenny Rogers (who contributed his vocal talents singing background on 'My Love') all made guest appearances. With an all-star cast and arrangements by Gene Page and James Carmichael, the album had everything going for it.

Everyone was duly acknowledged on the credits. Lionel's family, of course, came first, followed by a string of names, including Cal Harris (his engineer all the way from the Commodore days), Quincy Jones ("for phone calls, telegrams and words of wisdom"), Berry Gordy, the Motown family, and country producer Leland Rogers ("my spiritual adviser"). The final "thank you" was to The Commodores: ". . .my brothers, thank you for fifteen years of big fun."

The album, *Lionel Richie,* was all but complete when, in August, the man who had guided The Commodores' career died of a heart attack aged 54. Ashburn had been suffering from high blood pressure; according to one source who worked with The Commodores at the time, "the pressure of work had begun to take its toll on Benny. Then, when Lionel began to branch out on his own by getting his own attorney and working with Kragen, it definitely affected him. Benny had always been a stubborn kind of guy; he felt like he'd been a father to the group and, although he recognised that Lionel had seen a new direction for himself, he was afraid he wasn't going to be involved. In fact, he'd told the group that he was going to start working with other, new groups. You could tell that he was uneasy about Lionel's moves but, on the other hand, he knew it was inevitable. He just wasn't the same guy, he seemed to get tired easily and he just didn't have the enthusiasm anymore."

Co-workers described Ashburn as "stern, but very lovable, a man with a big heart, very down to earth and a lover of life." Industry colleagues called him "a tough negotiator, very protective of The Commodores." But whatever people said, it was clear that Benny Ashburn had been the mentor, the manager, the confidante of The Commodores: he had created a phenomenon out of his faith in the group's talent and he had stuck with them every inch of the way.

His death was devastating for everybody, as Lionel was quick to point out: "We came through this thing together and after all the terrible days of struggling to make a living we wanted to enjoy our

Lionel with Benny Ashburn, the group's manager, often referred to as the "seventh Commodore".

success together with Benny. He was like a father to us. We'd all phone Benny to find out what was happening and arrange to meet up. He was like the middle man that kept us all together. Communication was very difficult when, around 1978, we stopped living next door to each other in Tuskegee, but Benny kept us together as a family, for that's exactly what we were." Lionel dedicated the album to Ashburn "who brought six guys called The Commodores from the ground floor to the top of the world."

Lionel's 'Running With The Night' video gave him his first opportunity to act in front of the camera.

Tina Turner and Lionel duet together on 'Three Times A Lady' during Lionel's 1984 tour.

Lionel and Brenda at home in Los Angeles.

From left: Grandma Adelaide, Lionel, Brenda and Lionel's mother, Alberta.

93

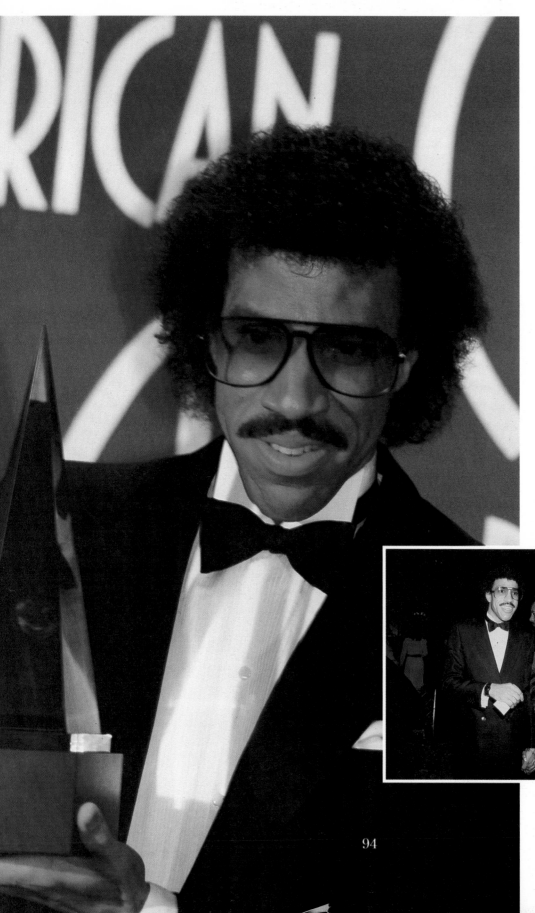

In February 1984 Lionel hosted the American Music Awards ceremony.

Lionel closed the Olympic Games in August 1984 with his hit song 'All Night Long'.

95

The gap left by Ashburn's death could not be filled easily and, with the imminent release of his first solo album, Lionel had some tough decisions to make. He went down to Tuskegee to sort out the problem with the group and they jointly decided on the appointment of Chuck Smiley, who gave up his prestigious job as Vice-President at ABC-TV to become The Commodores' new manager. Smiley, who took over as President of The Commodores' Entertainment Corporation, said that he saw a whole range of areas for the group to get involved with – "video, cable television and other non-music media – so breaking up the performing/recording cycle."

Rumours now began to circulate that, with the release of his album in October, Lionel was finally striking out on his own. With Ashburn gone, the one bond that kept the group together had been broken. "I'm in a strange position," Lionel admitted. "I want to make sure I don't step on these guys. We're not just a group of musicians, we're a family, and yet, at the same time, people are opening doors, pointing a finger at me. It's very frightening."

Brenda was there to offer emotional support, but Lionel still seemed uncertain as to what to do. He made no statement that he was definitely leaving, though casual comments made it hard to think otherwise. In a November '82 interview, Lionel reflected: "I think that the current Commodores' non-success has a lot to do with a lack of communication and co-ordination. There's a lot of competition, and getting six guys in the studio isn't easy when we're all doing different projects."

Aside from Lionel, other members of the group had been doing outside production work: Milan Williams worked with Dolly Parton's sister, Stella, and Ronald LaPread produced the group A Taste Of Honey. Neither project had the same impact as Lionel's outside production work, however, and the group had turned their full attention to the task of putting The Commodores back on top.

However, neither of the group's singles – 'Why You Wanna Try Me' (released in January 1982) or 'Painted Picture' (released in November of the same year) – which followed the successful 'Oh No' of September 1981, hit the bestsellers. The success of

Lionel Richie seated at the piano, on Saturday Night Live *in December 1982 – and with Terri Utley (Miss USA) and Karen Baldwin (Miss Universe).*

Lionel's first solo single contrasted strongly with the failure of the group's efforts, and Lionel's official split from The Commodores seemed imminent. Commodores' manager Chuck Smiley, responding to questions about Richie's future, stated that he had "no details I can provide at this time about Lionel's role in The Commodores."

It came as no surprise when, with the runaway success of 'Truly' (which hit the No.1 spot in the US on 23 October 1982), Lionel finally announced that he had assigned Ken Kragen to be his manager. Lionel commented: "With Benny gone, I knew I had a gap that had to be filled. Ken Kragen is one of the few people around with a real gift for management. I knew him and had worked with him so there was no question that he could do the job." By the end of 1982, with 'You Are' (the second single from Lionel's first solo album) in the Top 5, it was official: after all the speculation, Lionel Richie was now out on his own.

In subsequent comments, ever-conscious of the image he'd created with the media as a "good guy", Lionel was emphatic in stressing that not only had he made the decision to leave with great difficulty but that the split had, in the spirit of their long-standing friendship, been amicable. "When I did my album, it was designed to be a solo album and then I'd go back to The Commodores. They were thrilled to death about all this stuff happening to me but when you're talking about people who can do everything musically, you know they want their talents to be heard too. The group is at a stage where they want to test their individual skills and I understand that. It's deep water out there and they know all they have to do is make a phone call if they're in trouble."

Lionel, however, had not anticipated the international success his album would achieve. In the United States it sold over one million copies; it was a bestseller in the UK, throughout Europe, in Japan and Australia, racking up total sales of some three million copies internationally and spawning two No.1 hits. Lionel finally won his first Grammy award for 'Truly' — after seventeen nominations for his work with The Commodores, Kenny Rogers and Diana Ross.

In September 1983 he finally took to the road. The tour included some 48 dates and ended in December, after three weeks in the Far East. With the aid of manager Kragen – who had been told to "make [Lionel] a legend" – he was savouring the time "planning and putting [his] career together."

Rumours suggested that Lionel was actually afraid to step out on stage alone after fifteen years with The Commodores. "Sure, I get a little jittery now," Lionel admitted after a couple of dates. "I was a little jaded, almost bored, because of the routine I had gotten into with the group, and I find myself thinking now before I go on stage, 'What is it I'm supposed to do?' It's exciting, new, a challenge. But it was an insecure feeling early on in the tour to have just one limousine leave the hotel: I was used to three. It seemed strange to be the only one in the dressing-room when it came to changing into my costume for the night."

It also took Lionel some time to find the "right people" to go on the road with, musicians who "express the warmth of what I do and exude that feeling on and off stage." Lionel felt he had selected the perfect combination: "They were fresh, wonderful and very supportive." Lionel shared the stage with Greg Phillinganes, lead and rhythm guitar, and musical director for the group; Gerry Brown, drums, and former sideman with jazz star Stanley Clarke; Randy Stern, keyboards and vocals, who had played on sessions with funk group Cameo; Henry Davis, bass and vocals, from the group LTD; Carlos Rios, lead and rhythm guitar, and session player with Quincy Jones; and Sheila Escovedo, percussion and vocals. She ended up, as Sheila E, with a solo career and an international hit record in 1984, 'The Glamorous Life'. Lionel explains her attraction: "She's just great with audiences – she entices them and knows how to get them going! Brenda's the one who first saw her work and suggested she'd be a real asset for the band – she's been just that and, as the only woman in the band, we spoil her rotten, of course!"

The tour was a huge success. The first four dates in Lake Tahoe, Nevada, were in effect a trial run, and between two and three thousand people attended each show. Lionel remembers the night of the first show very well: "This was the very first time I'd appeared on stage without The Commodores and I was a little uptight. I walked out on stage and the crowd gave me a standing ovation. I couldn't believe it – I felt like I was home and it was wonderful." But until Lionel had played five or six shows he was unsure as to what to expect from his audiences. "I knew how many fans The Commodores had and, after leaving the band, I started to wonder, 'Am I doing the right thing walking out here by myself?' Then to have the crowd all of a sudden go, 'It's all right, Lionel, we're with you' – it really made a difference."

Broadway choreographer and director Joe Layton (who had worked with Diana Ross, Bette Midler and Olivia Newton-John, and won an Emmy for his work with Barbra Streisand) staged Lionel's show, advising him to open with the ballad 'Truly' with nothing but a piano as accompaniment. "For fifteen years, I was with a band that opened with three fast songs, bam, bam, bam. Now this guy was telling me to start out with a ballad, and no band behind me! He simply said, 'Lionel, trust me, it's going to work out all right' and, of course, it did. I had tears in my eyes for those first few shows: I was so relieved the crowd enjoyed me walking on stage by myself singing a slow song. It was really a terrifying moment for me at first because I had nothing to tell it would work."

The show included tracks from Lionel's solo album, ballad hits from the Commodore days – 'Sail On', 'Still', 'Three Times A Lady' – and an appearance by Diana Ross. This "appearance", as Lionel pointed out, was somewhat illusory: "On the show, Diana comes out of total darkness and for a minute the audience thinks she's really there." A life-size figure of Diana, projected on an enormous screen behind Lionel, had been given a three-dimensional effect by the lighting; while singing 'Endless Love', Lionel got "to gloat over her enlarged image and even attempts to hold hands with her!" in the words of one reviewer. Lionel noted the incredible audience reaction and said he was "terrified of what might happen if she showed up for real!"

Audiences everywhere reacted wildly to Lionel's performances. The first major show in Toledo,

Ohio, was a sell-out – with close to 10,000 people in the audience – as were the four nights at Radio City Music Hall in New York where The Pointer Sisters were the opening act. On the last night, Lionel added a midnight show as a benefit for three New York cultural organizations – The Actor's Fund, the Dance Theatre of Harlem and Symphony Space – commenting that "as my career grows and prospers, I'd like to put something back into the community."

As the tour hit different parts of the country, it gathered momentum, propelled by the chart success of Lionel's album hits. One reviewer declared it "hands down the finest live pop music experience of the year." Lionel also found time to spend with fans at different points during the tour; one incident in particular, in Chicago, left a strong impression on him. "We got a whole stack of mail in the dressing-room after we'd done this concert in October and I read a few of them and Brenda just kept reading. She found this one from a kid, Kenneth, who was in hospital paralyzed from a gunshot wound. Well, we got every single kids' game we could and stopped by the hospital and they really appreciated it. It made me realize what a blessing life is, and I'm determined to do some work with kids from now on."

Lionel also visited Tuskegee and played at Auburn University nearby; the Mayor of Tuskegee proclaimed 29 October 1983 Lionel Richie Day. "It was great; the town accorded me the ultimate honour – they put me on the front page of the local newspaper, and that has always been reserved for the Mayor."

Grandma Richie was seemingly unimpressed – "She just looked at me and said, 'Lionel Junior, go take the garbage out!' " – although she did show a great deal of interest in Lionel's chart positions! "It's really funny because she seems almost more concerned than I do about the way the records have been going and, when I'm home, she'll turn to me and say, 'We moved up a couple of places this week on the charts!' It's great to have that kind of support behind you, I must admit."

There is no doubt that Lionel's family is extremely proud of his success, yet, when asked what she thought about having a famous son, his mother was very straightforward: "I don't feel anything when

Lionel and Eddie Murphy backstage at Radio City Music Hall, October 1983.

people ask me how it feels to have Lionel as a son. That's just Lionel Junior – to me, he's just my son, not somebody famous."

But for audiences of all kinds, Mrs Richie's son was clearly famous no matter where he went. When Lionel took his show to Japan in December '83 audiences were just as impressed: "They don't speak English but they sing every lyric along with you, so you figure they understand, right? Wrong! When I'd say stuff like 'Did you like that?' there would be no response at all! Words like 'party', 'fun', and 'happy' are universal but, unless you're speaking Japanese, forget any long dialogue with the audience!"

Lionel was amazed at the composition of his audiences back home in the US, which seemed to consist of "eight-year-olds, mums and dads, grandmas, grandads, guys dressed in leathers and chains, Rastafarians – it's like the United Nations." His talent as a balladeer drew a very different audience from other contemporary black male vocalists, like Jeffrey Osborne, Luther Vandross and Peabo Bryson. Lionel noted that: "My records are going on the r&b and the pop charts at the exact same time; and the numbers are almost the same. That started happening as far back as 'Sail On' and 'Still'. Now, there are some black acts that have to be in the Top 10 on the r&b charts to get on to the pop charts at all – and sometimes they still don't get over. I've been lucky."

Almost the only other black vocalist with that sort of broad appeal was Michael Jackson, whose *Off The Wall* album also enjoyed r&b and pop chart success, a few years before Lionel's first solo album. It seemed, however, that the niche Lionel was carving for himself veered more towards the position that Johnny Mathis had attained as a middle-of-the-road song stylist, even though some of the material on Lionel's first album had a distinctive r&b slant. It was the white, middle-class American music lovers who comprised the bulk of the Richie audience, although black audiences were also familiar with his music. It wasn't until a year after Lionel's first solo album that his appeal became even more widespread as a result of the song 'All Night Long'.

Meanwhile, Lionel was adjusting to a new life-

avoid any change in his personality as a result of his international stardom. In subsequent interviews he talked about their relationship at length. "I couldn't stand being parted from her, so I made her my production assistant. We're always together now and I like to know what she thinks of what I'm doing at every stage of my career." He admitted: "We have had our ups and downs but we have never actually parted. If you are moving and going as fast as I have, you are bound to have traumatic periods. My home is where I tend to bring all my tensions, and Brenda is the only one who can help my transitions and my emotional periods. I'm amazed she's still here."

Although Lionel had people like Brenda and his manager Kragen with him every step of the way, he had some concern about how he'd fare as a solo artist. But by the time he hit the road in 1983 all his fears had been put aside. Within just one year, Lionel had established himself as a major superstar. He had won a whole array of awards – two from NAACP, two from the American Music Association, the Grand Prize Artist Award at the Tokyo Music Festival, and the People's Choice Award. He'd been featured on all major US television shows (including the famous Motown 25th Anniversary Show in February 1983) and he had made the cover of a great many popular magazines. His years with The Commodores had yielded album sales in excess of 12 million, but that achievement was dwarfed by the staggering acceptance Lionel's music received in the months to come.

Lionel and Brenda at home in Tuskegee.

style as a pop superstar. He and Brenda had moved out of Kenny Rogers' estate and bought their own mansion in the exclusive Bel Air section of Beverly Hills. With the trappings of national fame now in evidence in Lionel's life, the question in the minds of those who'd known him was whether Lionel would suddenly develop a huge ego. "Look," he protested, "I've been in this business for fifteen years now so my ego is the least of my problems. Everyone thinks I'm now enjoying instant success but that success has taken fifteen years."

Lionel credited the supportive relationship he and Brenda had created as the way he'd been able to

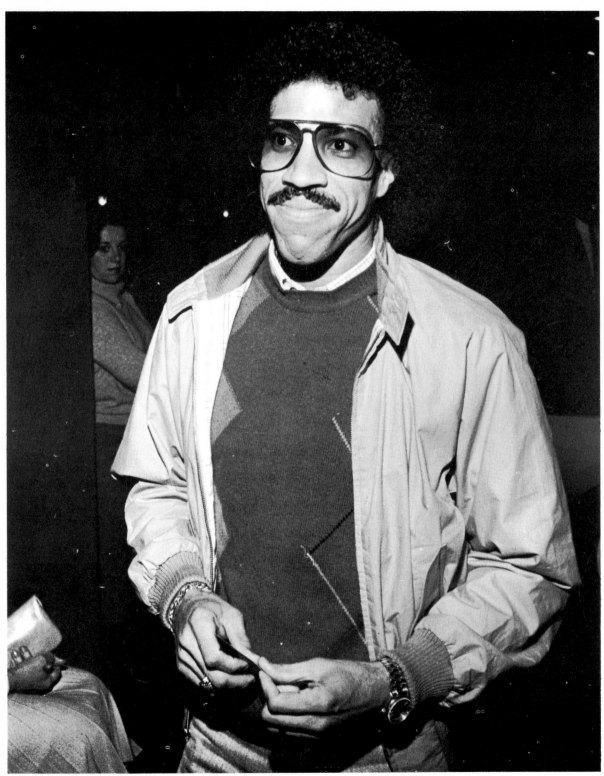

Lionel attends a dinner at the Beverley Hills Hotel, hosted by Big Brothers of America.

CHAPTER

CAN'T SLOW DOWN

Lionel's *Can't Slow Down* album, released in the first week of November 1983, spent over a year on *Billboard*'s Top 10 LP chart, mostly in the Top 5. It yielded a total of five US Top 10 singles for Lionel ('All Night Long', 'Running With The Night', 'Hello', 'Stuck On You' and 'Penny Lover'). It sold well over five million copies in the US and over one million in the UK, making it Motown's best-selling LP ever. This was no mean feat considering the sales of artists like Stevie Wonder, Marvin Gaye, Diana Ross, The Supremes and, of course, The Commodores – not to mention the host of artists like The Temptations and The Four Tops who'd had their share of gold albums through the years. Lionel made sure that the company's renowned founder, Berry Gordy, got the appropriate acknowledgement. "I spent time playing tennis with Berry during those early days and I had the opportunity to study a master. To be around someone like that can't help but inspire you." By the spring of 1984, Lionel's two Motown albums had sold a combined ten million copies internationally, the first racking up three million, the second an astounding seven million. The first hit from *Can't Slow Down,* the now-classic 'All Night Long (All Night)', had become the biggest-selling single world-wide in Motown's history.

As with his first album, Lionel started out with a wealth of material and he continued to write during production itself. He and co-producer Carmichael decided together on the final selection. Lionel explained the difference between the two albums: the first album, he said, was a bridge between his work as a Commodore and his work as a solo artist; the second allowed more room for adventure and risk. "It was really a departure for me and that was typified by 'All Night Long'. After some of my friends heard it, they were astounded – they just knew how different it was from what they'd expected me to do. That one song, 'All Night Long', was the first song I did that I consider to be truly universal. It seems like everyone loved it and related to it – people from everywhere."

So it was no surprise when producer David

Lionel – pictured here with Berry Gordy, head of Motown Records – accepts *special award for over two million sales of* Can't Slow Down

Wolper selected Lionel to close the 1984 Olympic Games with this song. Lionel performed before an estimated viewing audience of two and a half billion; he wrote a special additional verse for the occasion, and used nearly 200 dancers.

'All Night Long', with its infectious Caribbean lilt, nearly didn't make it to the album, however. "I recorded that and 'Running With The Night' at the very beginning of our sessions and then decided not to use them. I cut a lot more material for the album – which is usually how I work – and one of our engineers reminded me of the two songs and asked why we didn't include them. I'd really just forgotten about them, and so I went back and listened to them over again and, thankfully, we put them back on!"

The decision to include those songs was a fortunate one, since it provided Lionel with two hits in a row. He had a third hit with the wistful 'Hello', a song left over from sessions for the first album. Co-producer Carmichael had considered 'Hello' to be out of context with the rest of the album, but Brenda insisted that the song's beauty outweighed all other considerations.

Lionel and Carmichael once again employed the cream of musicians for the venture – people like Steve Luthaker and Jeff Porcaro from Toto, Greg Phillinganes, Paulinho da Costa, Michael Boddiker and Abraham Laboriel. They also harnessed the talents of some renowned co-writers: Cynthia Weil, one of pop music's most prolific writers, for 'Running With The Night'; and David Foster, producer and arranger extraordinaire, for 'The Only One'.

But it was Lionel himself who produced the album's biggest, most memorable hits – 'Hello', 'Stuck On You' and 'Penny Lover' (co-written with Brenda) and, of course, 'All Night Long'. He credited a good friend, West Indian-born gynaecologist, Dr Lloyd Byron Grieg, as his "dialect coach" on 'All Night Long' – the anthem that exhorted everyone to "party, karamu, fiesta, forever!" – noting that listening to Dr Grieg provided the "special" ingredient he was looking for. "He would come by the studio and I started listening to his accent. We got talking a lot and, when I was working on the song, I kept calling him asking him to talk to me! I knew I wanted to do something

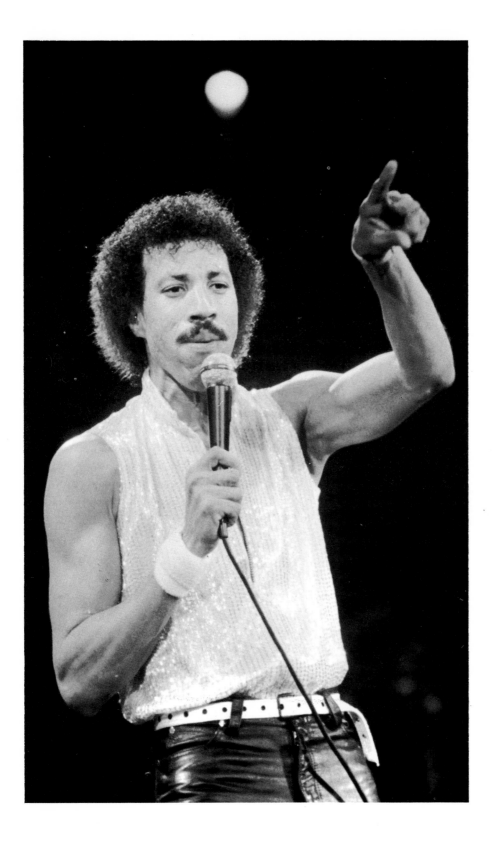

different for this record; when I found myself using some of his phrases, I knew I wanted to use his accent on the record. So I'd stop the musicians in the middle of a take and call him. I must have worried the guy to death – I spoke with him on the phone for almost two days!

"But the result was worthwhile and, when we recorded the song, the musicians just didn't stop playing – there's a good twenty more minutes of music on the original take. When it was remixed, you could hear the guys going real crazy – after a while, I just got up and left the room and left them to it." 'All Night Long' became Lionel's instantly recognizable theme song and it has received all kinds of acclaim. Stevie Wonder stopped midway through a performance in New York in October '83 to play the record to the audience, pointing out that it was his "favourite record". Singer Dionne Warwick opened and closed her show for almost a year with the song.

Lionel was a little more relaxed in his approach to the production of the *Can't Slow Down* album. "Kenny Rogers used to laugh at me, telling me that he'd get a whole album done in the time it took me to get just one line perfect! Kenny tends to be a little less intense in the way he deals with the whole business of recording an album – he's more into the feeling than the technical perfection of a take. So, for this album, I took his advice and really went for the feeling in each of the songs." And it quite obviously paid off: the emotion of songs like 'Hello', a huge international hit, seemed to touch people everywhere. But it wasn't simply the song that did it; Lionel had discovered the music tool of the Eighties – the video.

When Lionel began his crossover success with The Commodores, videos were hardly in use. By the time he went solo, videos had begun to take hold, and his first venture into the genre with 'All Night Long' – produced by Mike Nesmith (formerly of The Monkees) and directed by Oscar nominee Bob Rafelson – was a winner. The video captured all the excitement and energy of the song and was named one of the ten best productions of 1983, becoming one of the most heavily-played videos on the American MTV music channel. Initially, the chan-

113

nel had come under attack for its reluctance to feature videos by black artists; the acceptance of 'All Night Long' was evidence that Lionel had achieved a breakthrough into the rock market.

Lionel followed it with the rock-flavoured 'Running With The Night' video, in which he appeared as a slick, seductive, "street" guy, a change in image from the more sophisticated, "clean-cut" profile people usually associated with him. The record itself was not as successful as its predecessor on either side of the Atlantic, although Lionel believed in it sufficiently to contribute $80,000 of his own money towards the $200,000 it cost to make. The video was directed by Bob Giraldi (one of the medium's foremost directors) with choreography by Michael Peters (who had worked with Michael Jackson on 'Beat It').

But it was the emotion-filled video of 'Hello', also directed by Giraldi, which caught the public's attention on both sides of the Atlantic. Lionel played a lovelorn college professor attracted to a mysterious young blind student (played by Laura Carrington). The video revealed Lionel's as-yet undeveloped acting talent and assisted 'Hello' in becoming one of 1984's biggest hits world-wide. In Britain alone, the single held the No.1 spot for six weeks. The video of 'Penny Lover', Lionel's fifth single from the *Can't Slow Down* album, was released in September 1984; reportedly costing a small fortune to make, it hit the playlist of the American MTV channel almost immediately.

Lionel hosts the American Music Awards in LA in February 1984.

But for many of his fans, it was still Lionel's live performances which had the greatest impact. Not that being on the road didn't have its share of problems. In November 1983, Lionel's plane crashed on landing in Phoenix, Arizona, fortunately without injuring anybody on board. Although shaken by the incident, the musicians went on to perform that night as planned, Lionel momentarily becoming "ten times more famous when people thought I'd been killed in the crash!" But, fortunately, all tours were not marred by such dramatic incidents. "Sometimes," Lionel commented, "life on the road can be dull – especially after coming off stage, really energized and high from the audience's reaction, and getting into the confines of a hotel room. But I guess from all the years of experience I've learned how to turn my hotel room into a real exciting place with a stereo, keyboards – the whole thing. And I also don't stay in my room the whole time; I like to hang out with people, although these days that isn't always easy."

Lionel's fame of course has brought its share of problems: "You know, I'd like to be able to just drive around, go shopping, stuff like that, but it has become increasingly difficult. Not that I mind being with the fans because I know they are responsible for me being where I am. It's just that I can't do all the things I used to be able to do – even, say, going to the airport to pick up my parents where I can't risk going to the gate without starting a riot!" But he has learned to accept this loss of freedom as one of the

Lionel and Brenda with Marianne and Kenny Rogers at the Beverley Wilshire Hotel for the ASCAP Music Awards dinner.

hazards of superstardom. To get away from it all he either goes back home to Alabama and his family, where he can rest up without being bothered – particularly when "it's time to make important decisions and reflect on what's going on in my life and career" – or he "drives along the Pacific Coast Highway in California creating songs!"

Lionel's success has been accompanied by select media appearances. Tom Bradley, the Mayor of Los Angeles, declared 22 November 1983 "Lionel Richie Day". In February 1984, Lionel hosted the American Music Awards special, and the telecast of the programme, seen by millions of viewers across the US, won the highest ratings of any music awards show ever. "I've had nothing but compliments, not only from the public but from media and industry people as to how beautifully Lionel handled the show – so he's going to host the show again in 1985," commented Dick Clark, the show's organiser. Lionel's personable manner made him eminently suitable for the job, and he had the distinction of being the first black performer to host the national show.

Astute career moves continued to consolidate Lionel's position as a major star. He was named "ASCAP Writer Of The Year" by the American song licensing organisation. In March 1984, he won the Alumnus Of The Year Award presented by the United Negro College Fund – a tribute to his days as a student at Tuskegee Institute. In May, he was one of four celebrities at the Metropolitan Opera House's 100th Anniversary in New York – he appeared with John Denver, Yves Montand and Placido Domingo – performing 'All Night Long'.

In March, Pepsi-Cola announced that it had signed "the largest and most comprehensive agreement ever made between a performing artist and a corporation." The agreement called for Lionel to compose and perform a Pepsi theme song for a series of commercials to be aired that year; it also involved Pepsi-Cola in "film and television projects featuring Richie, in addition to joint support of charities of mutual interest." The soft drink company also agreed to sponsor Lionel's 1984 and 1985 tours to the tune of some $7 million; not surprisingly, Lionel said he was "looking forward to taking his

117

show on the road again, this time under the Pepsi banner."

The 1984 tour began in May. Lionel criss-crossed the country playing everywhere from Texas, Tennessee and Alabama to New Jersey, Illinois and Ohio. Every show was a sell-out and the tour had grossed several million dollars by the time it ended in August. Tina Turner opened for Lionel, providing her with major exposure to Lionel's audiences – they played to audiences of over 10,000 almost everywhere they went. She ended the tour with a No.1 single in the US, 'What's Love Got To Do With It'. Tina's raunchy, rock-oriented act contrasted well with Lionel's rather more conservative show, though when she joined him midway through his performance for a funky version of Rod Stewart's 'Hot Legs', he became less restrained. Their duet on 'Three Times A Lady' worked perfectly, and the show received rave reviews.

Not all the critics of course approved. Jonathan Taylor, reviewing Lionel's LA concert in July, found that "for all of Richie's virtues, good intentions and skill, there was something crucial missing from his performance. . .it had to do with guts and adventure. . .or, more accurately, lack of guts and adventure." But most people would have sided with Tom McCarthey, reviewing the show in Salt Lake City: "From the opening strains, Richie sang with sincerity and enthusiasm. His universal appeal was clearly seen with an audience ranging from wide-eyed youngsters to enthusiastic grandparents and every age in between. . .Lionel was just sensational."

In the two years since his decision to go solo, Lionel has captured the public's attention. But his success has not been matched by that of The Commodores. Lionel has this to say about their first post-Richie album, *13:* "It's a good beginning for them but they need an identity, a focal point. When I was with them, I was the lead singer and mine was the face of the group. I think "Clyde" should be prompted to be that face for them – he's a prominent singer and seems to be the strongest."

The album gave the group their first chance to produce themselves – without Lionel or long-time associate, James Carmichael – but it failed to achieve any great commercial success. This led

media commentators to note that, without Richie, the group were finished. Milan Williams says that when the group went back out on tour at the end of 1982 without Lionel, "people didn't know what to expect. . .they were anticipating what we'd be like." But a warm reception in Kingston, Jamaica, was followed by enthusiastic responses from audiences in Holland, the UK and France (where the group played at the Midem Festival in January 1983). In February and March 1984, the group did some dates in the US ("4,000-5,000 seaters," notes Milan) before trekking to Australia, New Zealand and Hawaii "for a great reception" in June. From July on, the group began working in the studio, but it had become clear that The Commodores needed to try some new musical direction rather than relying on the tried-and-tested formula that had worked for many years.

With the departure in November 1984 of Thomas McClary, new questions were raised about the group's future. McClary signed a deal with Motown and cut his first album for the company, with Lionel lending his support by singing background on the first single, 'Thin Walls'. In an interview with Steve Ivory of *Billboard,* McClary confessed that leaving the group "is a lot like leaving your mother; it's not easy to do," adding that he had actually begun to think about leaving the group in 1981. "I've been very open with the group about it and we started discussing the idea fully about six months ago."

The final decision to leave, he claimed, was brought on by the confines of working in a "democratic structure where everyone votes on everything. It's fine that everyone has a say on what we record, except that the group passed up most of the songs now on my own album. The more songs I wrote, the more I felt I needed an immediate outlet for my work. I'd watched the group pass up 'Lady' – which Richie wrote and which turned out to be a million-seller for Kenny Rogers. 'Thin Walls' from my album was written years ago and the group passed up that one too." McClary's comments highlight the sense of frustration that both he and Lionel felt about developing their creative talents as songwriters.

McClary in fact took a similar route to Lionel; he

119

worked on production assignments outside the group before finally leaving. At the start of 1984, he produced a Melissa Manchester session and scored a hit with r&b trio Klique's 'Stop Dogging Me Around'. He was prepared, so he said – "particularly from working with Richie and James Carmichael for all those years" – for the challenge of a solo career. "It was the easiest album I've ever done in all my years of recording – it was fun. I didn't want to lose my r&b roots. . .and I used some great musicians from the Los Angeles area."

McClary went on to admit that *13* had been less than successful and that the death of Benny Ashburn "was the hardest blow, no question about it. After Benny passed, we had to grow up fast and I'm not sure we ever did." He felt the group could bounce back to popularity "as long as they don't get below the quality that the public has come to expect" and that the addition of new lead singer J D Nicholas (a former vocalist with the group Heatwave) would help revitalise The Commodores. The group seemed open to changing their musical style. To this end the group used Dennis Lambert – who had worked with The Four Tops and Dennis Edwards, formerly of The Temptations – as producer on their most recent Motown album. Commodore Milan Williams reaffirmed this: "The group are re-emerging with a new sound. Apart from the hits we've had, we have always been basically a performance group, we expect to be right out there this year playing at those big stadiums and arenas again."

The Commodores are clearly looking to the future, not just holding on to the past, even though the possibility of a reunion with Lionel has been suggested several times by both parties. Lionel himself has said: "If what they do works, and if my stuff keeps working, then we can say 'let's blast people and both get back together again.' That's what I'd really like to see happen."

What Lionel has, in fact, seen happen has been increasing acclaim and recognition for himself. And, inevitably, more and more people are curious: who is this singer who, like Michael Jackson, has crossed all the barriers most black entertainers face in their struggle for recognition and acceptance? Unlike Michael, however, Lionel has not had to deal with innuendos about his sexuality, and his "good, clean, upright" image has helped him bridge the gap. Lionel is seen as a gentleman, a romantic; a faithful, loving husband; a guy who is humbled by his success.

In an attempt to quash this "too-good-to-be-true" persona, Lionel lamely confesses: "I have a tendency to stretch myself beyond the limits that are human or reasonable. For instance, there may be sixteen kids in the hotel lobby and I'll stop and sign autographs for them, then another twenty-four show up and I feel like I've got to please them too – meanwhile keeping someone somewhere waiting for me. So I'd like to learn to say 'no' a little more and to be able to do it with finesse. My other main fault is that I like to avoid confrontation as much as I can. When I feel my back is against the wall, I'll just drive off somewhere and come back later that day – the problems are usually still there waiting for me but I feel real good about having avoided them, if only for a short time."

Articles written about Lionel suggest he "doesn't touch drugs, refuses to swear, rarely drinks alcohol and prays every morning and evening." Despite his success, Lionel still holds strong religious and moral convictions. Any hints that he might fall prey to the attentions of lovelorn female fans are quickly repelled: "I don't have one-night stands. If I meet a girl I like, I might take her out to dinner and try to get to know her and that's as far as it goes. In fact, I've always been the guy who had trouble figuring out what to say to a girl after I said 'hello'. I've always found it difficult to deal with women on a one-to-one basis. But give me an audience of 8,000 and I'm fine."

Lionel's first tour in 1983 was very successful. He spent several months on the road, using The Pointer Sisters as his opening act; here he duets with June.

Lionel and Brenda at the UCLA campus for the annual SHARE party for charity.

Lionel greets the press at a party at New York's Club Area to announce his agreement with Pepsi-Cola; it is the largest and most comprehensive pact ever made between a performing artist and a corporation.

Brenda, who attends many of Lionel's press interviews and is frequently photographed with him, is quite well aware that her husband has become something of a sex symbol. It is perhaps inevitable, since Lionel continues to write songs with the specific intention of making people fall in love, that some of them should fall in love with him. "I sometimes read the letters he gets and I know that a lot of women want the kind of guy that his songs portray. . .but I hate to tell you this: in reality he's no romantic. It's all in his music. In fact, it's a trip getting him to say those three little words, 'I love you'. If he attempts it, he does it fast, running the words together or under his breath. So I just grab him and say 'Stand here and say it right out clear so I can hear it.' But he can't, so it all ends up in his songs. You see, the truth is he's one of the shyest people around – he can be the fun of a party but it's just a front for his shyness. What I like most about him is that he's kind and attentive and he's also very funny. And what do I do for romance myself? I have to listen to his records just like everyone else!"

Life for Brenda and Lionel is hectic, giving them little time to spend at home in their Bel Air mansion, although Brenda has reportedly been preparing for the couple's move into a new house in the same exclusive area. A foster father to six children, Lionel says that high on the couple's list of priorities is "starting a family of our own soon! We just have to make the time for it."

This shy multi-millionaire makes it clear that he doesn't regard his career simply as a means of acquiring more and more money. He is conscious, moreover, of his position as a role model for young black people, and he has participated in black community projects, particularly in the field of education. In June '84, Lionel donated $50,000 – matched by a similar donation from Pepsi-Cola – to a school program in Washington D.C. In addition, Lionel supports a number of charities including the American Cancer Society, The Juvenile Diabetes Association and SHARE. In an interview with *Jet* magazine at the time, he commented on his concern over mass starvation in Africa: "They send a camera crew over to walk around and film and they say 'Here's a good shot right here, here's a kid starving to death, look at his stomach.' And then, right here in the US, there are people starving to death and that's just horrible. . .I intend to use my music and money to help humanity."

Lionel views his music as a vehicle for "touching people's lives." He cites examples like the time "a lady pulled up at the traffic lights while I was waiting to cross the street." She told him how his songs fitted every aspect of her life, "all the ups and the downs." This acknowledgement, Lionel remembers, "just blew me away. What I like best about what I do is that I can be appreciated like that for my music."

With the exception of singer Sam Cooke, not since Nat "King" Cole has the crooner-style of singing gained the kind of mass acceptance that Richie has enjoyed – even as far back as the string of ballads he sang with The Commodores. He doesn't have the glamour and glitter of Michael Jackson, his former pillow-fighting friend from the road tours of the early Seventies (Lionel jokingly tells his audiences that he "taught Michael Jackson all the dance steps he knows"); the raw, erotic style of Prince; or the Latin sensuality of Julio Iglesias. He isn't a "rock star", he isn't flamboyant. His dancing is no threat to any of the breakdancers featured in his stage show, and Liberace needn't worry about his expertise as a pianist. Lionel's appeal lies simply in his songs and the way he sings them. The combination of old-fashioned romance and simplicity has proved a winner for the man who planned to be a preacher.

The solid background Lionel has had as a member of The Commodores, and his work in the past few years as a performer and recording artist, has assured him a place as one of the top male vocalists of the decade. His third Motown album is due very soon and is sure to surpass the success of its two predecessors. With sell-out concerts everywhere, records that have sold in their millions throughout the world, and an enviable collection of awards of all kinds, Lionel shows no sign of slowing down. And with a series of well-produced music videos behind him, Lionel's move on to the silver screen is inevitable. It would be no surprise to find him developing a stable of new artists, and he will doubtless continue his work producing songs for other established entertainers. Lionel Richie is certain to remain a dominant force in the entertainment industry for many years to come.

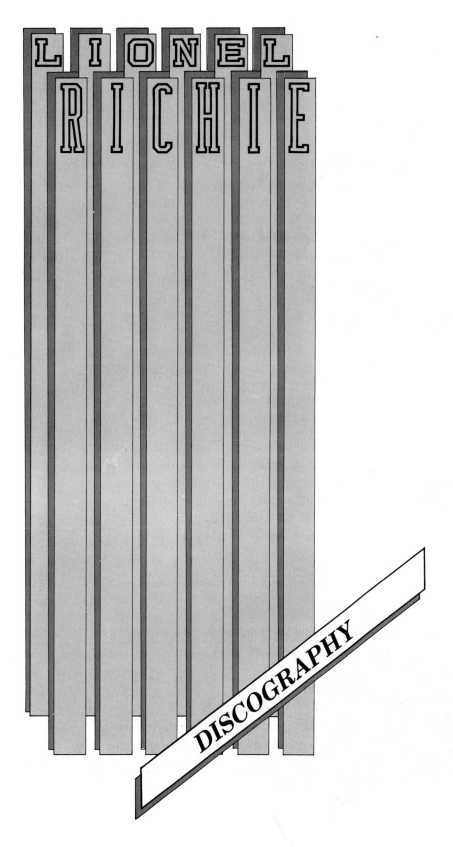

LIONEL RICHIE

DISCOGRAPHY

LIONEL RICHIE DISCOGRAPHY:

SINGLES	US:	RELEASE DATE & CHART POSITION	UK:	RELEASE DATE & CHART POSITION
With The Commodores:				
The Zoo (The Human Zoo)	MW 5009	3.72 (–)	TMG 924	11.74 (44)
Don't You Be Worried	MW 5038	1.73 (–)	—	—
Are You Happy	M–1268	8.73 (–)	—	—
Machine Gun	M–1307	4.74 (22)	TMG 902	7.74 (20)
Superman	—	—	TMG 935	2.75 (–)
I Feel Sanctified	M–1319	10.74 (–)	TMG 944	3.75 (–)
Slippery When Wet	M–1338	4.75 (19)	TMG 952	6.75 (–)
This Is Your Life	M–1361	8.75 (–)	—	—
Let's Do It Right	—	—	TMG 1007	10.75 (–)
Sweet Love	M–1381	11.75 (5)	TMG 1018	1.76 (–)
High On Sunshine	—	—	TMG 1034	8.76 (–)
Just To Be Close To You	M–1402	8.76 (7)	TMG 1127	11.78 (62)
Fancy Dancer	M–1408	11.76 (39)	TMG 1062	1.77 (–)
Easy	M–1418	5.77 (4)	TMG 1073	7.77 (9)
Brick House	M–1425	8.77 (5)	TMG 1086	9.77 (32)
Too Hot Ta Trot	M–1432	11.77 (24)	TMG 1096	1.78 (38)
Three Times A Lady	M–1443	6.78 (1)	TMG 1113	11.78 (1)
Flying High	M–1452	8.78 (38)	TMG 1127	6.78 (37)
Sail On	M–1466	7.79 (4)	TMG 1155	8.79 (8)
Still	M–1474	9.79 (1)	TMG 1166	10.79 (4)
Wonderland	M–1479	11.79 (25)	TMG 1172	1.80 (40)
Old-Fashioned Love	M–1489	6.80 (20)	TMG 1193	6.80 (–)
Heroes	M–1495	8.80 (–)	TMG 1205	9.80 (–)
Jesus Is Love	M–1502	11.80 (–)	TMG 1218	12.80 (–)
Lady (You Bring Me Up)	M–1514	6.81 (8)	TMG 1238	7.81 (56)
Oh No	M–1527	9.81 (4)	TMG 1245	10.81 (44)
Why You Wanna Try Me	M–1604	1.82 (–)	TMG 1256	3.82 (–)
Lucy	—	—	TMG 1282	10.82 (–)
With Diana Ross:				
Endless Love	M–1519	6.81 (1)	TMG 1240	9.81 (7)

SINGLES	US:	RELEASE DATE & CHART POSITION	UK:	RELEASE DATE & CHART POSITION
Solo:				
Truly	M–1644	10.82 (1)	TMG 1284	10.82 (6)
You Are	M–1657	1.83 (4)	TMG 1290	1.83 (43)
My Love	M–1677	4.83 (5)	TMG 1300	4.83 (70)
All Night Long	M–1698	9.83 (1)	TMG 1319	9.83 (2)
Running With The Night	M–1710	11.83 (7)	TMG 1324	11.83 (9)
Hello	M–1722	2.84 (1)	TMG 1330	3.84 (1)
Stuck On You	M–1746	6.84 (3)	TMG 1341	6.84 (12)
Penny Lover	M–1762	9.84 (8)	TMG 1356	10.84 (18)

ALBUMS	US:	RELEASE DATE & CHART POSITION	UK:	RELEASE DATE & CHART POSITION
With The Commodores:				
Machine Gun	M–798	7.74	STML 11273	9.74
Caught In The Act	M–820	2.75	STML 11286	4.75
Movin' On	M–848	10.75	STML 12011	11.75
Hot On The Tracks	M–867	6.76	STML 12031	7.76
Commodores ("Zoom")	M–884	3.77	STML 12057	3.77
Live!	M–894	10.77	TMSP 6007	11.77
Natural High	M–902	5.78	STML 12087	5.78
Greatest Hits	M–912	7.79	STML 12100	11.78
Midnight Magic	M–926	7.79	STMA 8032	7.79
Heroes	M–939	6.80	STMA 8034	6.80
In The Pocket	M–955	6.81	STML 12156	7.81
Love Songs	—	—	NE 1171	7.82
All The Greatest Hits	M–6028	11.82	STML 12183	4.83
Anthology	M–6044	9.83	—	—
Solo:				
Lionel Richie	M–6007	10.82	STMA 8037	11.82
Can't Slow Down	M–6059	10.83	STMA 8041	10.83